Praise for *The Influence Effect*

"I have long argued that business can no longer afford to exclude the strengths of half the human race: women. Leaders are slow to take us into that brave new world. But thanks to *The Influence Effect*'s intelligent approach, women can create their own path to power and start gaining the positions they want and need. I urge everyone to get a copy of this inspired and practical guide."
—**John Gerzema, CEO, Harris Insights & Analytics/The Harris Poll,** *New York Times* **bestselling author, social scientist, and speaker**

"Reading *The Influence Effect* is certain to remind a woman that 'power' is a verb and that she is the boss of her destiny. Well done."
—**Paula W. Hinton, Partner, Winston & Strawn, LLP**

"Women need to gain influence. *The Influence Effect* provides simple and practical tools to empower women to gain access to the C-suite."
—**Greg D. Carmichael, President and CEO, Fifth Third Bank**

"*The Influence Effect* might just change your life. The book tackles the age-old problem of too few women in leadership positions, and it does this in an utterly fresh, compelling way—by asking women to practice 'The Big Five Strategies' to pave their path to power. And as the real-world stories and case studies show, it works. I recommend this book to women everywhere who are ready to move forward faster."
—**Rich Karlgaard, Publisher,** *Forbes,* **bestselling author, award-winning entrepreneur, and speaker**

"The path to greatness is not a Machiavellian route of power; it is a trail of astute influence. And influence comes best from a confident, authentic spirit; a focused zeal to make a difference; and the wisdom of a set of strategies. *The Influence Effect* delivers all three. Written by four women who have successfully forged that challenging trail, this animated and thought-provoking book will give you a pragmatic map and crucial tools for your journey."
—**Chip R. Bell, author of** *Kaleidoscope*

"*The Influence Effect* tackles women's underrepresentation in leadership with cutting-edge research and expert insights. The result is a powerful guide with a clear message: women bring something very different—and needed—to the table. Designed to help women leverage their unique strengths as leaders, *The Influence Effect* can help women everywhere break through barriers to advancement."
—**Alyse Nelson, President and CEO, Vital Voices Global Partnership**

"*The Influence Effect* shows women how to start leveling the playing field by accessing power—faster, better, smarter. Don't wait to get yourself a copy. While you're at it, buy one for someone you know who may not fully recognize that women are our most underutilized resource for delivering our very best business outcomes."

—**Alden Mills, entrepreneur, Navy SEAL, and author of** *Be Unstoppable*

"Gender barriers won't ever go away, but if you follow the advice in *The Influence Effect*, they will no longer hold you back."

—**The Honorable Cari M. Dominguez, former Chair, US Equal Employment Opportunity Commission**

The Influence Effect

Other books by Kathryn Heath, Jill Flynn, and Mary Davis Holt

*Break Your Own Rules: How to Change the Patterns of Thinking
That Block Women's Paths to Power*

The Influence Effect

A New Path to Power
for Women Leaders

Kathryn Heath
Jill Flynn
Mary Davis Holt
Diana Faison

Berrett–Koehler Publishers, Inc.
a BK Business book

Berrett-Koehler Publishers, Inc.
1333 Broadway, Suite 1000
Oakland, CA 94612-1921
Tel: (510) 817-2277   Fax: (510) 817-2278   www.bkconnection.com

Ordering Information
Quantity sales. Special discounts are available on quantity purchases by corporations, associations, and others. For details, contact the "Special Sales Department" at the Berrett-Koehler address above.
Individual sales. Berrett-Koehler publications are available through most bookstores. They can also be ordered directly from Berrett-Koehler: Tel: (800) 929-2929; Fax: (802) 864-7626; www.bkconnection.com
Orders for college textbook/course adoption use. Please contact Berrett-Koehler: Tel: (800) 929-2929; Fax: (802) 864-7626.
Orders by U.S. trade bookstores and wholesalers. Please contact Ingram Publisher Services, Tel: (800) 509-4887; Fax: (800) 838-1149; E-mail: customer.service@ingrampublisherservices .com; or visit www.ingrampublisherservices.com/Ordering for details about electronic ordering.

Berrett-Koehler and the BK logo are registered trademarks of Berrett-Koehler Publishers, Inc.

Printed in the United States of America

Berrett-Koehler books are printed on long-lasting acid-free paper. When it is available, we choose paper that has been manufactured by environmentally responsible processes. These may include using trees grown in sustainable forests, incorporating recycled paper, minimizing chlorine in bleaching, or recycling the energy produced at the paper mill.

Library of Congress Cataloging-in-Publication Data

Names: Heath, Kathryn, 1949– author.
Title: The influence effect : a new path to power for women leaders / Kathryn Heath
[and three others].
Description: Oakland, CA : Berrett-Koehler, [2017] | Includes bibliographical references and index.
Identifiers: LCCN 2017028471 | ISBN 9781523082766 (hardcover)
Subjects: LCSH: Women executives. | Women in the professions. | Influence (Psychology) | Leadership. | Leadership in women. | Career development.
Classification: LCC HD6054.3 .H43 2017 | DDC 658.4/092082—dc23 LC record available at https://lccn.loc.gov/2017028471

First Edition
22 21 20 19 18 17   10 9 8 7 6 5 4 3 2 1

Set in Arno Pro by Westchester Publishing Services.
Cover design by Adrian Morgan
Interior design by Laurel Muller

*To the generations of
amazing women leaders
who have and will change
our world for the better*

Contents

Foreword

This is a book that needed to be written, and it's a book that needs to be read. Influence is not a nice-to-have in business; it is a nonnegotiable. Influence depends on having a seat at the table and entails having your voice shape decisions and outcomes. Not enough women are influencing today. It's true that too few of us "sit at the table," especially in the C-suite. In order to get there, stay there, and make real contributions at every step, we women need to do some things differently.

We need to ensure that what we say gets heard. This sounds obvious, but it is not easy. Getting heard requires preparation and practice on our part. Men and women communicate differently. Women tend to use more words, speak more formally, and focus on process versus outcomes. There is nothing wrong with that, but because it's not how men communicate, men often tune such speech out, which means that your input may not be appropriately considered.

At one point, I met with a male colleague to discuss how to have his team sell a technology product that my group developed. His first words, before I'd said a thing? He asked, "Why should we sell your product?" I wanted to explain the client relationships it would help them build, the best-in-class product attributes that took years to develop, and the product's superiority to anything our competitors have. Instead, I said, "Because it will add $40 million to your revenue goal for this year." He heard that! I knew he was thinking primarily about how he and his team could be successful, so I spoke his language.

Disagreements cannot be taken personally. Sometimes we confuse influence with getting everyone to agree. In reality, influence is getting the right decision made even when people do not agree. We need to quit trying to please everyone. We must be able to make a decision and say, "Here is why X person and Y person disagree with me, but this is what we need to do anyway." We need to quit relying solely on agreement and consensus and instead show we have a point of view and can stand by our decisions. One of my female colleagues is confident enough to say occasionally to her boss, "Just because you disagree with me doesn't mean that I am wrong." We must become comfortable with disagreement.

Confidence must come from within. I learned this lesson a while ago, and I've never forgotten it. I was at a public event being introduced as the incoming board chair of a large nonprofit. The person introducing me spoke enthusiastically about my warmth, approachability, and sense of humor. He talked about the heart I bring to my decisions and how fully engaged I am in my community activities. I sensed that description of me would surprise colleagues in the audience who only knew my office persona. When I took the microphone I said, "Yes, that was me he was talking about, in case you couldn't tell!" A few days later, my boss at that time gave me some feedback: "Cathy, people who work with you in the community love you, but not everyone at the bank loves you like that. Figure out what is different when you are in the community and see if you can bring that person to work." That was hard for me to hear, and it was one of the most important pieces of feedback I've ever received.

I realized I was giving myself permission to be my authentic self in the community, but at work, I was behaving in ways that I thought I *should* behave. I was imitating the behavior of others, and I did not feel confident unless I had the approval of others. Since then, I have made it my mission to show up with confidence and to be my true self. I have found that influence and authenticity are inextricably linked. Only by being truly self-confident can we influence others to follow us. And remember, influence is a nonnegotiable for leaders.

What works for men at work does not necessarily work for women. This book was written so that you, too, can connect your influencing skills with your authenticity. My hope is that with practice, greater self-awareness, and the knowledge gained from the insight and experiences highlighted throughout this book, you will become a person of greater influence and you will make a difference.

Cathy Bessant
Chief Operations and Technology Officer
Bank of America

The Influence Effect

INTRODUCTION

The Politics Problem

W E'RE GLAD TO BE BACK! We've been busy since the 2011 publication of our first book, *Break Your Own Rules: How to Change the Patterns of Thinking That Block Women's Paths to Power.* Since then, we've spoken to hundreds of women and men at conferences, we've led workshops and seminars, and we've coached many women who are breaking rules and are on the path to becoming senior-level leaders.

Break Your Own Rules described the six patterns of thinking that create career barriers and proposed new rules that enable us to break free from limiting beliefs and achieve the career momentum we need to succeed. The book became a *New York Times* best seller. It resonated with scores of women, and it has remained a relevant part of the current dialogue as women continue to strive to reach the top of organizations.

In *Break Your Own Rules* we introduced our "Red Suit Vision," which we remain fully committed to in all of our work:

> *We have a dream. It is a big vision...it is a leap...and it is audacious: we want to see women make up at least 30 percent of all top leadership positions in corporate America by the year 2025. We believe that 30 percent is a tipping point. When 30 percent of corporate leaders are women, the goals and direction of corporate America will change. The old rules will be shattered. America's corporations will be better led, and everyone will benefit.*

1

That dream is the reason we wrote this book: *to further advance our vision and offer a new path to power for women.* Although many things have changed since we published our first book, some others have remained the same. As women, we still need advice and coaching that is geared specifically for our career needs and experiences. That one thing can make all the difference in our success. There are so many of us, perhaps like you, who work hard, make sacrifices, and bring considerable talent to the table. To most of our colleagues in business, we are star performers. We work long hours and are accustomed to success. And yet, sometimes our careers get stalled or derailed. We lack support, make innocent missteps, and are blindsided by the fallout. That's exactly what happened recently to one of our clients, Sara.[1]

> *Earlier in her career, Sara finished graduate school and joined a promising start-up, where she helped negotiate its sale to a much larger competitor. She made a quick pivot to a medium-size telecommunications company and gradually rose through the ranks. She managed a P&L and helped the company ride out the 2008–9 recession by being one of the people involved in several innovative new product offerings and acquisitions. Not only was she great with clients, but she was also a rainmaker. More recently, she was asked by the CEO to sit on the executive leadership team.*
>
> *That's when her career momentum slid to a halt.*
>
> *Almost right away, she felt as if her colleagues on the leadership team weren't hearing her. She left leadership team meetings feeling blocked and frustrated. She felt increasingly powerless and ineffective. The final blow came a year or so later when she was passed over for a promotion she wanted immensely and felt she legitimately deserved based on her track record.*
>
> *Sara had been appreciated by her peers and respected in her role, and she'd generated considerable upward momentum in her career. Where did she go wrong? According to her boss, Sara needed to learn to better maneuver through the politics of the upper echelon. We were asked to coach her, and her 360-degree feedback offered us some insight into how we could help. It indicated that Sara lacked political savvy and was unable to influence*

others. More specifically, "she has established numerous relationships, but has not gained the support of key peers. She expresses her ideas, but is unable to do what it takes to persuade other leaders. She 'manages up' well, but she so far has been unable to bring her colleagues on board with her agenda." She did not know how to cultivate support for her ideas or deal with resistance from peers. Her response to us was, "I'm smart. My ideas have merit. Why do I have to do all of this politicking?"

Sara's story is familiar to us because we hear stories like hers again and again. The reality is that barriers become tougher for us to overcome as we approach the highest levels of leadership. That's when organizational politics becomes most intense. There are reasons for this, but the single common denominator we have found across all our work is this: *what works for men at work doesn't work for women.*

Parsing the Politics Problem

When we ask groups of women who have read *Break Your Own Rules*, "Which positive pattern of behavior is hardest for you master?" one has always been the clear winner: being politically savvy. It turns out that most of us are not actually motivated by unbridled competition. We do not gravitate toward backroom deals or trading favors. Instead, most of us value collaboration, inclusion, and win-win outcomes.

We have written about women and office politics for the *Harvard Business Review* and numerous other publications. The last major article we wrote for *HBR* was based on a research study we undertook in 2013.[2] As part of that study, we conducted surveys with over 270 female managers in Fortune 500 organizations to determine what they liked and disliked about business meetings. One of the things that repeatedly fell into the dislike column? Navigating politics.

In our sixteen-year process of coaching and training female leaders, we've maintained a running list of common threads. The disdain of office politics comes up repeatedly. Political obstacles are the top barrier women mention to us in our everyday work. In addition, in reviewing several thousand 360-degree feedback reports, we found that a notable number of female executives and their managers cited becoming politically savvy as an ongoing development need for women.

Although *office politics* has both positive and negative connotations, we define it as the strategies and tactics that people use to gain advantage, sell their agendas, and earn support from colleagues. Even when we view it in these straightforward terms, we see that women struggle to determine where they should aspire to be on the continuum shown in Figure 1.

On one hand, they have gotten to where they are because of hard work, and they do not want to be perceived as "overly political." On the other hand, they see instances in which outright "political maneuvering" and ruthless behavior have paid off for some of their colleagues. We urge women to consider the middle ground.

In 2015–16, we conducted another round of research. This time we wanted to understand why women were so turned off by office politics. We surveyed 134 senior executive men and women in leading organizations (see Appendix B), and the results shed a surprising light on the high barriers women face along the journey to career success. First, when we asked men and women who was better at office politics, women were more than four times as likely to say that men were better than women than they were to say

FIGURE 1   The Office Politics Spectrum

Just
Work
Harder

Be a
Ruthless
Politician

Be
Politically
Savvy

FIGURE 2 A Perception That Men Are Better at Office Politics

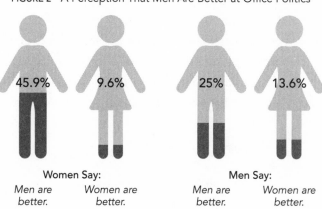

Women Say:

Men are better. *Women are better.*

Men Say:

Men are better. *Women are better.*

that women were better, and men were nearly twice as likely to agree that men were better (see Figure 2).

It was an eye-opener for us to learn that both men and women thought men were more innately skilled at office politics.

Additional survey results, combined with follow-up interviews, revealed that the overall degree of difficulty for women maneuvering political situations at work is much higher for the following reasons:

- Women and men *define* politics differently.
- Women are *judged more harshly* than men when engaging in office politics.
- *Lack of access* to sponsors puts women at a disadvantage.
- Women and men have *differing approaches* to power and influence: collaboration versus competition.

This book, *The Influence Effect*, moves women past the politics problem and offers a new path to power. It's more than a path—it's a runway because it frees women to take off in their careers on their own terms. *The Influence Effect* will work for women, not because gender barriers will no longer exist but because they will no longer hold us back.

Before moving on to our core ideas about women and influence, let's look at what else the numbers revealed about office politics. Our research findings, we believe, are not just surprising and enlightening, they are also instructive. We have used them to develop actionable strategies that help women bridge the influence gap, leverage their strengths, and use influence as a tool to succeed at the highest levels of leadership.

What We Have Learned

Our survey and executive interviews form the basis of this book and inform our prescriptions. Here's what we found.

Women and men define politics differently: Women manage relationships, whereas men are more transactional

Our survey results reveal that 76.6 percent of men and 68.2 percent of women are united in their overall dislike of office politics (see Figure 3).

FIGURE 3   The Majority of Us Dislike Office Politics

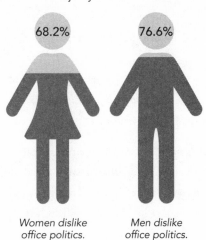

Women dislike office politics.   *Men dislike office politics.*

However, although men and women generally agree on their disdain for office politics, our follow-up interviews indicated that they *disagree* on the overall *definition* of politics. For example, women were far more likely to mention "developing relationships and ideas," and men were more than twice as likely to describe "immediate influence" and "carving a one-time advantage."

For example, David Holt, managing partner at HBW Resources, told us, "Politics is a set of tools people use to further their own agenda." Similarly, Frank Forrest, chief risk officer at Fifth Third Bank, said, "Politics helps us gain a strategic advantage." Many other men used similar words to describe how politics helps them. The women we spoke with looked at politics in a different light: Margaret Spellings, president of the University of North Carolina, former president of the George W. Bush Presidential Center, and former U.S. secretary of education, told us, "Politics is about maneuvering human interactions." And Betty Thompson, executive vice president and chief personnel officer at Booz Allen Hamilton, said, "Politics is a natural part of building any relationship." Consistently, men told us that politics is about *winning* and women said politics is about *building.*

According to our research, men are direct and systematic in how they think about political situations. They go for the quick victory and move on. Women think about the impact over the long term and anticipate cumulative results. This difference in targeted execution may mean that women spend more time and effort on politics and the payoff is less immediate.

Women are judged more harshly than men

The clear majority of men and women in our survey said that women are judged more harshly than men when they use the tools of politics (see Figure 4).

Respondents resoundingly acknowledged that biases and stereotypes are still ingrained in both men and women, and they drive unconscious behaviors, which in turn perpetuate work environments that undermine women. Because stereotypes and implicit bias work against our success, women expend energy trying to be perfect at politics, yet the overall degree of difficulty in achieving success is much higher for us.

FIGURE 4   Women are Judged More Harshly Than Men

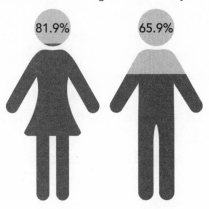

Women say: Men say:
Women are judged more harshly than men.

From Our Study: Women Are Judged More Harshly Than Men
"People still think women are 'manipulative' and men are 'focused' and 'results-oriented.'"
    —KATHY RIDGE, CEO, LEVRIDGE RESOURCES

"If a woman is aggressive, then she is labeled with the 'B' word. Both aggressiveness and manipulation are more easily tolerated in men."
    —CHRIS HECK, VICE PRESIDENT AND CHIEF INFORMATION OFFICER,
    DUKE ENERGY

"There is a double standard. There is a narrow line for women."
    —FEMALE SENIOR EXECUTIVE

"When men are aggressive they are viewed as 'powerful.' When women are aggressive they are labeled as 'pushy.'"
    —MIKE RIZER, HEAD OF COMMUNITY RELATIONS, WELLS FARGO

Melissa Koskovich, senior vice president and director of corporate communications and marketing at the American defense company Leidos, told us, "If a woman asks for a favor in the workplace, she can be perceived as needy or calculating. For men, it's just another quid pro quo swap, 'I owe you one.'" Bob Sprague, president and CEO of PCI, a marketing firm in the Washington, DC, area, agreed, telling us, "If women are competitive, they can be tagged unfavorably. It's a much greater challenge for women in political situations at work." If these comments sound extreme, they aren't—the top executives we surveyed and interviewed were in full agreement and speaking on the record.

Lack of access puts women at a disadvantage

Our overall findings suggest that women believe that being politically savvy is crucial to advancement in their careers. According to our interviews, this may be due to the fact that women are still fighting for a place at the table. The women we interviewed talked freely about being blocked from opportunities and access. Men agreed. Because there are so few women in leadership positions, it is much more difficult for women to gain access to the support relationships, sponsors, and opportunities they need to get promoted. The research on the power of sponsorship for women is copious and deep. Sponsors are essential to career growth, no question.

According to Cathy Bessant, chief operations and technology officer at Bank of America, "If there are fewer women at executive levels, then there are fewer people for us to connect with." Bessant acknowledged that this puts women at a major disadvantage when they are trying to sell their ideas, build a consensus, or get promoted. Mike Rizer, head of community relations at Wells Fargo, put it this way: "Maneuvering political situations is just one more barrier to advancement for a woman. Why? There are fewer senior female leaders for them to connect with."

Women and men have differing approaches to power and influence: Collaboration versus competition

The majority of men and women in interviews said that men and women have differing approaches when it comes to applying office politics. More women

mentioned using empathy and collaboration, whereas more men mentioned being competitive and taking risks. Neither approach is right or wrong, as each of
us is unique, but the female paradigm may work against us in some cases. For
instance, one important study suggests that the underrepresentation of women
in academia reflects a systemic bias against them *when they collaborate with men*.[3]
The study found that when women coauthored research with male counterparts, men received most of the credit. Given the emphasis women in our survey
placed on collaboration, this may further decrease their chances for success.

In general, the men and women we interviewed believed men had a greater
propensity to compete in the office setting. Chris Heck, vice president and
CIO of Duke Energy, told us, "Men are more overtly competitive and aggressive than women," and Frank Forrest, chief risk officer at Fifth Third Bank,
agreed, saying, "Men have more of a competitive spirit and are willing to use it
in political situations. It's in their biology." Meanwhile, Alicia Rose, Deloitte &
Touche global lead client service partner for American Express, said, "I can't
tell you how many leaders have said to me: 'When I was looking to promote
someone into a key position, I had four male colleagues at the door proactively
pushing their experience, yet I had to spend three hours and six phone calls
convincing female candidates they were ready for the job.' "

Finally, women told us they had no desire to model their leadership style on
one that was more aggressive and less collaborative. It was very important to
them to avoid "violating their values" by changing to be more like men.

The Influence Effect

These differences and barriers illustrate how difficult it is for us, as women,
to succeed in a business environment that is male dominated. In this book,
we talk about the high "degree of difficulty" for women at work. It is like the
diving competition at the Olympics: the degree of difficulty on some dives is
much higher than on others. What is different here is that even when we, as
women, use the same moves as men—being smarter and more prepared than
anyone else at the table, for instance—it is still more difficult for us to be judged

objectively. When it comes to politics in the workplace, double binds and barriers make it harder for us to succeed.

Political savvy is a skill like any other, and we can learn to use it to break down barriers. Yet we propose a different avenue altogether for women to break those barriers. Our main premise, throughout this book, is that we gain more from our efforts when we focus on *achieving influence* as opposed to *playing political games*. We therefore propose a new system, a new approach, a new paradigm. *The Influence Effect* will move us past playing political games and on to using the strategies of influence to get our voices heard, create powerful connections, and drive our agendas.

Instead of playing on a field that is forever tilted against us, *The Influence Effect* helps us to even things out and enjoy the panoramic view we so richly deserve.

We are redefining the rules here, and we hope you will join us. This book is about creating a way for women to finally play *all out*. This is a game in which both men and women can participate at their chosen pace. We have different sensibilities; we see situations differently, and for the most part we go after them in our own way. We don't need to engage in tactics that have a mostly male slant. Instead, we can use the tools of influence to create a better way for women.

About the Book

This book is organized into three parts that explore and explain our framework (see Figure 5).

Part 1, Prepare to Influence, sets the stage for the balance of the book in several ways. First, it describes what we have learned about influence, including why it is an ideal tool for women and why it is a skill that can be practiced and ultimately mastered to help us rise farther and faster in our careers. It also prepares us to influence by presenting a process to help us factor personal strengths, values, and goals into our influence journey. It goes on to explore how to appraise external factors such as industry changes and big

FIGURE 5   Igniting the Influence Effect

picture context. Finally, part 1 guides us to assess the existing hierarchy and networks within our organization to accumulate the baseline of knowledge and intelligence we need to get started.

Part 2, Practice: The Big Five Strategies, lays out five powerful strategies that we use in our coaching work. Separately, each of the Big Five strategies represents a smart, effective way to sell your ideas and drive change; together, these strategies enhance each other and create a cumulative force for influence.

Chapter 4, "The Power of the Informal," helps us work behind the scenes to gain support from colleagues and strengthen our relationships using informal networks and power. Chapter 5, "Relationship Maps," show us how to look around and identify key stakeholders—decision makers, influencers, and adversaries—to secure strategic connections that make political maneuvering less complex. Chapter 6, "Scenario Thinking," helps us identify the nuanced options in a situation, remain two moves ahead in the political process, and manage the dynamics of gaining formal support when it matters most. Chapter 7, "Influence Loops," is a systematic approach for enrolling others in our ideas, bringing them on board, and getting their buy-in—and doing it over and over. Finally, chapter 8, "Momentum," describes how to use early wins to create a tipping point of support as we begin to accumulate influence.

The Big Five strategies are designed to work together, making the whole greater than the parts. They can also be used à la carte to help us overcome resistance, remain agile, and achieve influence as everyday situations arise.

Part 3, Influence in Action, utilizes two common scenarios to demonstrate how these influence strategies play out. First, we look at how to overcome resistance to pave the way to gain support for our agenda. Second, we show how to succeed "on the corporate stage"—in meetings in which we need to use influence to sell our ideas and ourselves, every day.

Influence is a result of effort and practice. It is a skill all of us can acquire. Some of us believe that influencers are born with their talents fully formed, but we strongly disagree. We make it our mission in this book to pave the way and provide methods to help you develop influence. With that, you will be prepared to achieve your goals on your own terms.

Sara, the executive we described at the beginning of this book, turned her situation around to become one of our favorite success stories. We frequently mention her to other women we coach because she used the tools in this book to knock down barriers and become a highly influential leader. She did this by practicing and mastering the skills and strategies we introduce in the pages that follow.

To begin, let's take a closer look at influence itself and why we believe it is the best path to power for women.

Chapter Elements

➟ Stories from women we have coached

➟ The unwritten rules you need to know

➟ The limiting beliefs that hold you back from achieving influence

➟ Questions for reflection to help you pause, reflect, and move ahead

➟ Strategies you can use to achieve influence

PART ONE

PREPARE
to Influence

1

The Influence Effect

*Power is a tool, influence is a skill;
one is a fist and the other is a fingertip.*

—NANCY GIBB

IMAGINE YOU'RE ON THE BEACH watching a group of men and women surf. It's a sunny day and the wind is whipping while the beach warning flags snap in a rhythm. There are rip currents in effect and most people keep close to shore, worried about the dangerous conditions.

You watch the surfers chatting and laughing in the water as they wait for their wave. Two surfers approach a wave and decide it's not big enough. Another group paddles toward the largest wave in the set; they deftly jump on their boards and grab what looks like the best ride of the day. You marvel from the shore—how do they make it look so easy, graceful, and even fun? Surfers will tell you that it takes practice and a large dose of courage. They understand how to factor in overlapping elements seamlessly to achieve the ride they want. Expert surfers can see a wave approaching and calculate how many seconds they have before it will break. They can spot a wave that will break gradually, so they can ride across the crest as it slowly closes. Experienced surfers look like artists, masters of their craft.

This dynamic is what we want for women. We want you to become masters of influence. Like surfing, or any complex endeavor, achieving influence as a leader is seldom simple. It requires practice to master the skills, and experience to perfect the timing and execution. Also, like surfing, influence requires an awareness of what's happening below the surface to accurately size up the situation.

Unlike surfing, understanding influence is mandatory for anyone who wants to sell his or her ideas and aspirations to others. Influence—*the capacity to impact agendas and outcomes and bring other people on board*—is ultimately the tool people use to get things done. All of us know influencers: we see them in action every day and we take note. Some influencers are the change agents and transformational leaders of our organizations; others are the subject matter experts and technical specialists. Still others are the bold problem solvers who cut through complexity and ambiguity. The truly influential individuals among us demonstrate enviable talents that fuel and sustain their success. These are attributes such as executive presence, confidence, determination, passion, empathy, and the ability to build trust. Regardless of what influence looks like or how it is accomplished, it is without a doubt a key component in career success for all of us as individuals and leaders.

Our objective throughout this book is to describe the strategies of influence and tailor them for women. We believe influence is the best tool we can use to break past the gender barriers that many of us experience as female executives.

Our original research, combined with our experience training and coaching over thirteen thousand female leaders over the span of sixteen years, has shown us that *greater influence* equals *greater advancement*. We have found that influence, for women, is a proxy for the formal power only a few of us have achieved.

That's why we've written this book—to give women the skills they need to succeed at the highest level. Our research showed very clearly that women believe that influence suits their leadership style. The women we interviewed did not recoil from influence as they did when they talked about office politics.

This draws on a thread that connects all our findings: what works for men at work *won't work for women*. When we try to apply advice created by men and for men, it doesn't feel right to us. In the same way that wearing a business suit designed for a man is uncomfortable for a woman, listening to ill-fitting, poorly tailored advice creates friction and slows us down. This book eliminates the friction by introducing five key strategies that women can use to achieve influence on our own terms and in our own time.

The Influence Effect: Why It Works for Women

Bridget, a regional director at a real estate development firm in Detroit, told us why she works hard to cultivate influence. In her own words, "It keeps me moving ahead in my career and I use it as a lever to drive change."

A few years ago, Bridget wanted to completely revamp the key processes for how her company interfaced with clients. It was an ambitious undertaking aimed at disrupting, and vastly improving, a sales infrastructure that had been left in place for decades. Part of the plan was to reshape the leadership team to hasten the information flow and streamline decisions so that deals could get done quicker. She spent weeks working the numbers, designing a business case, and practicing her pitch.

"Those initial actions were just the table stakes," Bridget told us. "The far more difficult and tedious test was clearing the political landmines that were buried across the organization."

Early on in her effort, Bridget was confronted by two powerful colleagues who had a vested interest in preserving the status quo. There were others, as well, who might choose to align against her to block the path to change, but Bridget acted with determination.

Throughout a two-month period, she met with every decision maker separately. She adapted her plan numerous times. She negotiated with each faction to account for their objections. She courted and eventually won over the skeptics and found the right message to neutralize the two entrenched critics. Ultimately, she made the formal pitch to the board and the idea was implemented. When the new structure was finally rolled out across the business units, it must have looked as though Bridget simply jumped on her surfboard and took off. But that's not the way it worked.

As she told us, "What most people saw happening was the result of a well-orchestrated influence campaign that occurred below the radar." In short, influence must be cultivated. It may not be easy at first, but with practice you can become a master.

The *Influence Effect* is the phrase we use to describe the positive lift that we, as women, experience as we use influence to make our voices heard, create powerful connections, and drive our agendas. The Influence Effect creates a ripple that amplifies our words and actions, attracts followers, and creates a new path to power for us.

A first part of delivering the Influence Effect is reframing the office politics discussion to eliminate the emotional baggage of the phrase "office politics" and put it into a new conceptual frame that suits the style of women.

Many of the women we coach, and those we've interviewed, believe that practicing "office politics" may imply that they are being "Machiavellian or inauthentic." Christi Deakin, a Wells Fargo executive, agreed with the consensus, saying, "The word *maneuvering* sounds negative or dishonest." We need to increase our power and be more politically savvy, the women acknowledged, but office politics did not register with them as the right tool.

This reframing is necessary to help us move beyond the negative mind-set and practical limitations that are associated with office politics. As Kathy Ridge, CEO of Levridge Resources, told us, "Influence aims at shared goals that are in the organization's interest. Whereas, politics often seems to focus purely on individual rewards." Likewise, another client of ours told us, "I prefer to engage in influencing as opposed to practicing pure politics, because I view influence as positive and transparent."

This practical reframing helps us break past the politics that our research told us holds women back. This is an important prerequisite that sets us up for success; yet it is only part of understanding why cultivating influence works so well for women. We found that the Influence Effect elevates women for several important reasons.

1. Influence suits our leadership style

Women should never need to act like men in order to succeed as leaders. Cultivating influence allows us to win at work while remaining true to our chosen leadership style and code of conduct. In our research, for instance, we heard that many women want a relationship-based approach to success. We won't generalize that all women are alike, but many told us they don't feel the need to chase quick political wins. Instead, they work to achieve success in ways that are subtly different. Their adrenaline is primed by going after bigger-picture, qualitative objectives such as building trust, cultivating strategic relationships, and steering change and reform. In short, influence helps women focus on the following:

- Collaboration over coercion
- Cumulative advantage over quick wins
- Inclusion over zero-sum gains
- Change over status quo norms

2. Influence can be actively cultivated

Many of us feel sidelined in our careers because we are uncomfortable engaging in political maneuvering and power plays. Another roadblock is the enduring gender stereotypes that hold us back from advancement. Focusing on achieving influence puts the power to act back into our own hands. It keeps us actively engaged and advancing toward our goals. Even better, influence can be learned, practiced, and perfected using the Big Five strategies we present in the following chapters.

3. Influence is a tool for the times

Organizations are flatter, less hierarchical, and more matrixed than ever. In an age in which collaboration trumps individual interest, the use of influence suits our needs far better than political maneuvering and power plays. Influence creates deeper connections and better access points and enables us to advance in our careers in new and better ways. Similarly, influence is all about reaching out to others and cultivating strategic relationships. The women we coach are drawn to using influence because it helps them move ahead with their agenda despite complexity and ambiguity.

4. Influence creates a new way to work

Perhaps the most important reason we are making the case for influence as a tool for women is that it is a path to change and progress. Although women hold 52 percent of all professional-level jobs, American women lag miles behind men when it comes to their representation in leadership. As of 2017, we hold only 5.8 percent of CEO posts in Fortune 500 firms[1] and just 19.9 percent of board seats in the Fortune 500.[2] In high tech, women represent a mere 30 percent of the workforce,[3] and that percentage plunges when you examine the makeup of the management ranks.[4] In academia, far fewer women than men are awarded tenured positions each year.[5] The list goes on and on. In every industry, from private equity investing to network television, women are underrepresented at the top and we are paid less throughout our careers for the same work. We can cry foul about the data, and yet it is far more difficult to find a solution to this enduring gender divide. That's why we have written this book.

Now, let's step into the water and begin riding the waves.

Executive Summary

- Influence is a key component in career success and advancement for women. It can be a proxy for the formal power we have yet to achieve.
- Influence helps us focus on cumulative advantage over quick wins, inclusion over zero-sum gains, and change over status quo norms.
- Influence is a skill that can be learned, practiced, and mastered using the five strategies we will explore in this book.
- The *Influence Effect* is the phrase we use to describe the positive lift that we, as women, experience as we use the tools of influence to make our voices heard, create powerful connections, and drive our agendas.

2

Think Bigger, Aim Higher

Tell me, what is it you plan to do with
your one wild and precious life?

—MARY OLIVER

Anne headed marketing for the education division of an e-learning company. For eleven years, her job was to work with school systems to provide customized interactive materials to improve student performance. Anne had a reputation for being creative and energetic, and she earned the support of several key leaders, including the chief marketing officer (CMO), who hired her and was her direct supervisor.

Over the years, Anne became comfortable in her job; she earned a bit of autonomy for herself and created a lifestyle with predictable hours and the ability to work from home. She liked her job and even recalled a time when she felt poised and ready for bigger and better challenges at the company. But more recently, every time she thought about making a change or sponsoring a new project, she froze. She wanted to dream big and be dynamic, but she wasn't even sure what that might look like. To make matters worse, the company had become mired by bureaucracy, which led to lackluster results in Anne's unit.

After two years of sluggish sales, the board demanded action. The CEO fired the CMO, and Anne's comfortable life was turned upside down. The new CMO reorganized the division and hired three new marketing executives. Anne found herself reporting to a new boss, instead of directly to the CMO. The new boss treated Anne as if she were part of the problem instead of part of the solution. Anne was stunned and felt as if she were being punished.

Anne tried to remain positive, working hard to win over her new boss. She put forward new ideas, but she couldn't gain any traction. Anne was left wondering, what happened here?

Like many of the women we coach, Anne lost sight of her career goals for a time. She was talented and achieved enviable success, but then she hit a wall and became complacent. Anne did not have the time or the energy to make change happen for herself or for her department.

Anne's story typifies the challenge many of us face when we first wade into higher levels of leadership: we fail to think big. It is hard work! Anne aimed low and stuck with the status quo instead of creating the change she knew needed to occur. As a result, the change happened *to her.*

THE UNWRITTEN RULE: Bigger Really Is Better

Let us coach you for a few minutes. Close your eyes and visualize yourself achieving everything you want for yourself professionally. Allow your mind to imagine two or three possible paths for your career. To make this exercise easier for you, we will add two conditions. First, you *cannot remain in your current position.* You must do something different, bigger, with broader impact. The second condition is this: no matter what you choose to do, *you cannot fail.* This is good news! Get busy and visualize some options for yourself. What would they look like? What would you be doing? Think bigger. Aim higher. What is the secret career goal you haven't told anyone? What do you really want for yourself?

Thinking bigger is critical for several reasons.

1. ***It delivers big ideas.*** Big thinking signals change—it generates action. It gets us beyond the here and now and forces us to think about the future. Thinking bigger is associated with solving big problems and achieving big dreams.
2. ***It helps us attract followers.*** Big ideas are engaging and exciting. They inspire others to join our cause and they brand us as visionary leaders. People admire and follow individuals who are brave enough to imagine a bold future instead of thinking small.
3. ***It leads to bold decisions.*** Once we train our brain to think bigger, our lofty vision serves as the filter for future decisions. Thinking bigger helps us proceed courageously and dynamically.

Thinking bigger and aiming higher sets us up to have options and the courage to pursue them. Yet, this is admittedly challenging in a complex world in which we can easily become paralyzed by uncertainty and ambiguity. Like Anne, we need to summon a great deal of courage in order to supersize our thinking.

LIMITING BELIEFS That Lead to Small-Time Thinking

Many of us admire big thinkers, but we seldom see ourselves in that role. Why is that?

Limiting beliefs in women stem from multiple sources. One source is outdated gender stereotypes that box us into traditional gender roles: "Women are not supposed to be ambitious"; "Women should be nurturers, not leaders." Limiting beliefs also originate in the dark place within ourselves where self-doubt and denial reside. In our work with women leaders, we focus on coaching women to replace the limiting beliefs they harbor about themselves with positive messages. We can learn to funnel our energy in a positive direction. All of us can take steps right now to change our limiting beliefs.

Before moving full steam into the specific tools that women can use to think bigger, let's look at three common limiting beliefs and start to set them aside.

"I'm not naturally strategic."

"I can't think of myself as big."

"I'm an impostor."

"I'm not naturally strategic"

A 2009 study by INSEAD professor Hermina Ibarra revealed that female leaders were superior to their male counterparts on many leadership and performance measures but they fell significantly behind in one key area: vision.[1] In our coaching conversations, we hear that women feel more comfortable *implementing* vision than formulating it and selling it to others. As one woman told us, "It feels easier to keep my head down and get the important work done. Setting the larger strategic agenda is a different matter altogether."

This type of thinking reveals a confidence issue that has massive career implications. It's no surprise that a study of more than forty-seven thousand global leaders found that the biggest single differentiator between top management and middle managers was their strategic vision.[2] Having strategic vision is a critical competency. Part of the disconnect for women may be a style issue. Women tend to be *collaborative* and work to create a consensus around big ideas as opposed to owning them themselves. While there is no doubt that female executives have big-picture vision, the challenge is giving ourselves permission to speak up and enroll others in our visions.

"I can't think of myself as big"

One of us was coaching a young partner at an engineering firm. She was striving to gain traction as a leader and struggling to articulate a career path for herself. When pressed to think broadly and articulate an ideal future for herself three to five years out, she was stumped. "I can't think of myself as big," she said. "I feel stuck in the moment and I can't envision landing in a larger role."

This type of limiting belief is common. Most of the women we work with feel stuck at one time or another. There's no question they are committed to building their careers, but everything from office politics and financial pressure to commitments at home and anxiety about world events can make them feel trapped in their current circumstances. Their careers can sometimes become unstuck on their own, when things inevitably calm down. Other times, people benefit from an intervention from a coach or mentor.

It's vital for women to aim higher and envision a future state for themselves. A male executive friend of ours said, "You have to be able to outrun your headlights." He meant that we need to see ourselves beyond the here and now. If we don't see ourselves as "big," no one around us will.

"I'm an impostor"

A coaching client of ours, Karen, fell victim to her limiting beliefs six years ago. Karen is a CPA and an accomplished partner at a large accounting firm. She had provided outstanding service to many medium-size and large clients over the years. However, when the firm nominated Karen as a candidate to be an engagement partner for a large and prestigious blue-ribbon client, she faltered. Karen was one of the two outstanding candidates that the firm was proposing to the client. The audit committee of the client's board would interview both candidates and choose the one they thought was the best. Karen confided in her coach that she believed she was "not a good match" for the job. She had a litany of concerns, both rational and otherwise: "I am not as sophisticated as the board members on the Audit Committee. I get nervous in interview situations. I'm not good at small talk. I'm sure they will not pick me."

Karen felt like an *impostor.* She believed that she was not as good as the firm said she was and that the audit committee would see right through her. After that, the firm would know she had been "faking it" all these years, and that would be the end of her career.

The *impostor syndrome*, a term coined by clinical psychologists Pauline Rose Clance and Suzanne Ament Imes in 1978, is a phenomenon in which very accomplished people are unable to believe and accept their own accomplishments. They believe they have "fooled" others into thinking they are more competent than they really are.[3] Many successful women fall victim to the impostor syndrome, but it is a somewhat rare phenomenon for successful men.[4] One reason is that the parameters of success in contemporary society are biased toward men.[5] According to *Psychology Today* writers Satoshi Kanazawa and Kaja Perina, "Nobody recognizes women who are successful in female terms. So, part of the problem may be definitional."[6]

Karen worked hard with her coach to rid herself of the extreme limiting beliefs. In preparation for the interview, she spent many hours reviewing information about the client and its history with the firm. She also worked on executive presence—right down to clothes, jewelry, and makeup—which was of particular concern to her. She even practiced entering the boardroom, shaking hands, managing introductions, and making small talk. All of this helped to build Karen's self-confidence.

Most important, Karen worked on her psyche. With her coach's help, she began to notice the negative thoughts she had about herself. She learned to catch herself when her inner voice told her something irrational, untrue, or belittling. Gradually, Karen learned positive thinking and self-talk.

When the day before the interview arrived, Karen called her coach. We asked her, "Are you feeling ready and prepared for tomorrow?" Karen answered, "Yes, I'm definitely ready. I feel great about my preparation and I feel great about myself as a candidate. I am convinced that I can do an outstanding job for this client. If they don't pick me I can handle it, but I know *they would be lucky to have me.*"

Karen faced the impostor syndrome head on and put it behind her. We were delighted to see her conquer her limiting beliefs. For the record, the audit committee chose her as their new engagement partner, and she was a noted success in the role.

Questions for Reflection

➡ How do you orient yourself to "think bigger"?
What negative messages are you telling
yourself?

➡ Close your eyes and visualize yourself doing
something "bigger" with your career. Can you
describe what you see and write it down?

➡ Now, have you got some big ideas? Who can
you share them with?

STRATEGIES for Thinking Bigger and Aiming Higher

Regina works in a pressure-cooker environment. She assists states in setting up multi-million-dollar disaster recovery projects and emergency response systems that enable the distribution of critical funds, program monitoring, and oversight that complies with federal regulations. It's a highly complex job that saves lives, and Regina thrives on it. Yet it didn't start out quite like this. Regina made it happen by thinking bigger, aiming higher, and courageously steering her career.

As a resident of Metairie, Louisiana, in 2005, Regina was distraught as she witnessed the widespread devastation delivered when Hurricane Katrina crippled the region. As part of the New Orleans metropolitan area, Metairie was in the epicenter of the storm. At the time, Regina was an oil and gas consultant for a big professional services firm, focusing on business opportunities in the Gulf Coast region. When she looked around following the storm, all she saw was stagnation.

"Nothing was moving. Not trash, not water, and especially not the money parishes and townships needed to start the long road to recovery."

Regina was pleasantly surprised when her firm asked her to be part of a three-month project to help the State of Louisiana begin to make their disaster recovery efforts more efficient. She knew very little about government contracts and public works risk assessment. But she did understand how to connect the dots between problems and processes. She thrived in crisis situations and had a talent for finding solutions.

Regina saw a big opportunity to make things better. "We couldn't speed up the trash pick-up ourselves or return people to their homes," she recalled, "but we could find a way to get billions of dollars into the right hands faster."

Regina and her team created a process to make government recovery funds available within ten days of a request. It was a dramatic improvement that required thinking differently. The bureaucratic roadblocks were significant, and there was potential for misappropriation of funds.

The twelve-week engagement stretched out to three years, and every second was a roller coaster ride. By then, Regina was hooked on the mission. The project was an aha moment for her, and she had no intention of returning to everyday management consulting.

Regina had a big dream, and she turned it into a vision to build a new practice at the firm that focused on crisis management and recovery.

For Regina, thinking bigger and aiming higher were pivotal steps along the path to achieving influence. For all of us, achieving influence requires that we have a bold vision to guide our actions. There are five strategies that we use with our coaching clients to help them create and sustain lofty visions.

STRATEGIES for Thinking Bigger and Aiming Higher

1. Nurture your vision.
2. Check the weather.
3. Train your brain.
4. Cut the grass.
5. Embrace your passion.

1. Nurture your vision

Now that you have been practicing thinking bigger, you are getting close to creating a bold career vision for yourself. Don't let go of it. Don't tell yourself all of the reasons it *won't* work. Your vision may be somewhat blurry or vague right now, but if you continue to nurture it, it will develop into a clear picture that guides your behavior and your decisions.

So how do you nurture your vision? First, you need to share that vision with others. One of the reasons we lose out on jobs and assignments is that we don't declare our interest. If you have a bold vision, you need to tell people about it. The more you do that, the better you will become at making your case and enrolling others in your cause.

To nurture your vision, you must step outside your comfort zone. You must take the risk of owning your big idea before gaining full consensus from the group. You may need to stand firm when your ideas are challenged. In Regina's case, she put her career on the line. She told us, "If this doesn't work, I'll need to leave the firm and reinvent myself."

Nurturing your vision also requires the courage to act. As women, we need to communicate our vision without resorting to *over*analysis. Many of us are armed with reports, case studies, and rigorous financial modeling. Are these things important? Sure. Can they sometimes be crutches that slow us down? Definitely. Nurturing your vision requires the courage to know when to set aside the PowerPoint slides and simply say what you believe in.

Similarly, nurturing your vision requires leaving your emotional baggage behind. One of the things we've learned through our coaching is that many women take adversity personally. But remember, being a change agent invariably leaves battle scars. You *will* meet resistance and you *will* have to overcome obstacles. When your ideas are voted down or can't get the attention of key leaders, don't take the setback personally. This is all part of your career process.

2. Check the weather

Now that you have a vision, you must remember to "check the weather," again and again. Think of it this way: If your vision is to drive from Cincinnati to

Chicago, you will do a lot of checking before and during your trip. You will check the weather forecast. You will make sure your car is tuned up and filled with gas. You will pack clothes, food, and other supplies.

Checking the weather in a business setting is similar. While keeping your destination (your vision) foremost in your mind, you must simultaneously look for all external influences and obstacles that could impact your progress. What is going on with your customers? What about budgets? How does your vision coincide with overall company strategy?

Checking the weather is different from vision, because vision places emphasis on a single desired outcome. It is also distinct from strategies, which are the approaches we use to achieve our desired outcome. We advise checking the weather continually, because external forces can alter our options and perceptions. Checking the weather keeps us moving forward. It helps us navigate uncertainty and steer our path successfully. The executives we interviewed for our research overwhelmingly emphasized the importance of having a "panoramic view" of the journey, not just a narrow focus on the destination.

Regina's vision was her ultimate dream of building a practice around crisis management and recovery. The moment she envisioned and identified this goal, she started checking the weather repeatedly. She encountered the initial challenge of creating a process for delivering funds in the aftermath of Hurricane Katrina. She managed the ongoing bureaucracy during the extended recovery process for New Orleans and beyond. She factored in the implications of the American Recovery and Reinvestment Act of 2009 and how the legislation might impact her grand plan. She also considered the trillions of dollars in government grant money and how that would be the basis for building a business case within her firm.

Regina told us that focusing purposefully on checking the weather enabled her to achieve her vision. It guided her in several ways, including the following:

- AS A FILTER TO GUIDE HER DECISION MAKING. Regina checked the weather when making strategic decisions that advanced her cause.

When she was offered a position back in traditional consulting, for example, she was able to take a pass without experiencing misgivings because she knew the role would not take her where she wanted to go.

- AS A TOOL TO HELP HER SELL HER BIG IDEA. Checking the weather helped Regina "see" the idea and describe it to others. She could articulate not only her vision for a new practice but also the potential obstacles and how she planned to route around them.
- AS A WAY TO NAVIGATE AMBIGUITY. Checking the weather gave Regina the confidence she needed to believe in her vision. It also allowed her to change strategies as surrounding events developed. Regina remained agile as staffing, budgeting, and funding ebbed and flowed, because checking the weather forced her to envision various options and contingencies.

3. Train your brain

Vision requires grit and resolve, and we know that women have these things in reserve. Yet, gaining influence and leading change are lengthy endeavors, and setbacks come with the territory. In order to help manage the leap-of-faith aspect of thinking bigger, we use a few thought tools to help us sustain our momentum.

As events change, remember to pause and adjust your approach. Ask yourself, what strategic adjustments must I make to remain on course? Making subtle changes in your *actions* helps sync your strategy with current realities, and making small shifts in *thinking* will help you remain relevant and realistic. And both of these will help you keep your message current as you sell your agenda to colleagues.

Practice shifting timeframes. What happens if a major career opportunity presents itself sooner than expected? What will you need to do to be ready? How will you react if your plans are sidelined due to office politics or budget constraints? What are your contingency plans? Considering various timing alternatives periodically will help keep you vigilant and resilient.

Finally, we suggest looking at your vision through multiple lenses. When Regina looked at her plan through a business lens, she articulated it in this way: "I want to build a new practice at my firm around crisis management and recovery." When she examined it using her personal values as the lens, she thought about it in another way: "I want my work to make a difference to people who need help." Examining your vision through multiple lenses—business objectives, career, personal values, and so on—is yet another way to make your big dreams attainable.

4. Cut the grass

Much of the work we do to help women think bigger and aim higher amounts to mental boot camp. It takes considerable resolve to develop the type of confidence, resilience, and situational awareness that leadership and influence require. Our final assignment for flexing your mental muscles amounts to metaphorically cutting the grass.

Ideas require time to marinate. Some of us run on the treadmill or sit by the ocean when we need to stop and reflect. One of our clients goes outside and cuts the grass.

Cutting the grass means taking time to unplug from the rush of our day-to-day lives. We need to turn away from e-mail, smartphones, and meetings to think and reflect. Our brains need time to reboot. Our reflection model is simple and powerful: Do. Reflect. Learn. Most of the time we are busy rushing from place to place without pause. *Cutting the grass* means intentionally taking time out to reflect. Through reflection, we learn. Through learning, we discover what is working for us and what is not working so well. Reflection and learning are the keys to helping us adjust our strategies so we can direct our momentum toward achieving our vision. Only through reflection and deep thinking can we mindfully plan for the future. Escape from the rush and cut the grass!

5. Embrace your passion

We know that Regina's vision was a labor of love. She said it was much more than a job for her. Hundreds of people worked with her in crisis management and recovery, and most moved on before she found the right core team of people who could help her build a sustainable practice. The common denominator across the team, she discovered, was shared passion. We see this in our work coaching women to think bigger. Our own passion is built on our vision that more women leaders at the top will make business better and everyone will benefit. What is your passion built on?

Passion, confidence, and the ability to think big are some of the starting points for achieving influence. All of these are internal factors that propel us forward and allow us to begin to build the infrastructure we need to develop and grow in our careers. In the next chapter, we will examine some external prerequisites along the journey to fostering the Influence Effect.

Executive Summary

- Failing to think bigger and aim higher is a misstep many of us make when we move into higher levels of leadership.
- Several things drain our influence and power: being perceived as "less strategic" than men; falling victim to the impostor syndrome; the inability to see the immense potential in ourselves and our careers.
- Nurturing a bold vision requires getting unstuck, thinking bigger, and sharing your vision openly with others.
- "Checking the weather," or looking around our environment to consider context and outside factors, vastly improves our planning and delivers better outcomes.
- Making strategic adjustments, shifting timeframes, and looking at our end goal through multiple lenses are ways we can train our brain to think bigger.
- Taking time out for reflection (or "cutting the grass") helps us be resilient and maintain perspective.
- Passion needs to be a part of our purpose and what propels us to achieve influence.

3

Construct Your Scaffolding

Sticks in a bundle are unbreakable.

—KENYAN PROVERB

Linda was ambitious. Her dream was to become the first female partner at the elite industrial design and architectural firm where she worked. The wheels were in motion, and there was little question in her mind that it would happen. Her boss had singled her out, groomed her, and assured her that the promotion was all but inevitable.

Getting to this lofty perch had been no walk in the park for Linda. She worked hard in college and completed a top master's degree program in two years. She went on to become an intern at the firm, where she worked long hours for low pay. She completed the grueling state licensing exams, passing on her first try. The firm could see that Linda was a rising star, and they hired her as an associate.

She continued to work lengthy hours, including nights and weekends. In time, Linda grew weary of the dizzying pace, year after year. After a time, she found herself mired down by the lack of a clear career path and the crazy hours. Linda knew she needed help. Fortunately, she found a strong advocate to help her advance: Ed, her boss and a senior partner. Ed took an interest in Linda's career and began mentoring her. She worked closely with Ed over a period of years, attending to his clients and acting as his right hand during deal negotiations. She even managed Ed's top client—the firm's largest account.

Ed showered her with ongoing praise and continued to assure her that he was the only sponsor she needed, saying, "I'm your way in. You're going to take on my clients and be my replacement when I retire. It's a done deal."

Then the unexpected happened. Without warning, there were some "organizational changes" and Ed's retirement became imminent. Linda heard the news at the same moment everyone else did, in a company memorandum. Although she was surprised that Ed was retiring so soon, she wasn't particularly worried. She and Ed had a long-standing agreement. She had done her part and he had worked it all out…right?

Unfortunately, multiple events transpired at once. First, numerous senior partners stepped forward with mentees and protégés of their own, whom they hoped to promote when the spot opened up. Next, it became clear to Linda that Ed never made their plans explicit to the other partners. He never fully secured their buy-in, and none of the others knew Linda especially well. Finally, Linda received word from the partnership committee that she was being deferred as a partner candidate for that year. Yes, Ed was replaced, but not by Linda. Linda eventually resigned to accept a more promising role at another firm.

THE UNWRITTEN RULE: Construct Your Scaffolding

It would be easy to blame Ed for his role in Linda's career debacle. Yet, Linda herself admitted to us that she had done very little to proactively manage her own future. Her biggest mistake was relying on a single sponsor and naïvely waiting in line for her big promotion.

In our work coaching women, we use *scaffolding* as a metaphor to describe how each of us must create our own access to opportunities and advancement. Our scaffolding is the lattice of support that we put into place around ourselves, from sponsors and advocates to peers and family members (Figure 6).

FIGURE 6   Where Is Your Scaffolding?

Scaffolding supports us, gives us the confidence to think bigger and take chances. It helps us grow and increases our options exponentially.

Several women in our study mentioned the importance of surrounding oneself with trusted support. One C-suite executive put it this way: "Getting ourselves in a position to achieve support is critical for success. We need like-minded allies by our side."

As Betty Thompson and so many other women told us, you can't develop influence without support scaffolding—period. Once again, we would argue that the degree of difficulty in attaining that support is higher for women than men for several reasons.

FIRST, THERE ARE FEWER WOMEN TO PULL US UP. Research shows that leaders tend to promote people who look and act like them. In other words, men in positions of power are more likely to promote other men. At a time when only 5.8 percent of chief executives in the S&P 500 are women,[1] we are much less likely to be pulled up by the collar into leadership positions. Less face time with top leaders and less trust both make gaining access and achieving influence more of a challenge for us. It's more difficult for women to establish support for these same reasons.

NEXT, WE MUST FORGE OUR OWN PATH TO LEADERSHIP. With fewer role models and peers than men and less experience in executive leadership, it's more difficult for women to decode the rulebook and identify a path to the top. In our research, one female C-suite banking executive put it eloquently: "Women feel like there is a 'behind the scenes' that they are not part of." Linda relied on a single supporter, Ed, to guide her along the path to becoming partner. She never sought additional input or asked others if Ed's perspective was on target. She needed more information to accurately crack the code to becoming partner. She needed to gather input, understand the promotion landscape, and work strategically to create her own access to the next opportunity.

FINALLY, THE HIGHER UP WE GO, THE LESS FEEDBACK WE GET. Fully 68 percent of the senior-level women in our previous (2013) study said they seldom receive any helpful feedback about how they perform in professional settings, even when they ask. One male executive in our study admitted, "We talk about them, but not to them."

Research in 2016 by McKinsey & Company and LeanIn.org corroborates our findings and experience. They found that women receive informal feedback less frequently than men—despite asking for it more often—and have less access to senior-level sponsors.[2] This means that our access to opportunities and information is blocked, and we interact with senior leadership less, making it more difficult to sell our ideas and advocate for ourselves. Men have their scaffolding up all the time; it's a part of the traditional business landscape. Women need to construct their scaffolding strategically in order to access top

> **What We Heard in Our Interviews**
>
> *"It's just more natural to have those critical career conversations when you are with same-sex people. Those conversations happen mainly outside the office, so this is about access and comfort. Men can have those conversations more easily with each other."*
>
> —MONIKA MACHON, FINANCIAL SERVICES EXECUTIVE, AIG (RETIRED)
>
> *"There are still so few female role models at the top of the house. When there are more women sponsors, there will be easier access and a natural assumption that we can get there."*
>
> —ANNE M. STAROBIN, GLOBAL HEAD OF EXECUTIVE LEADERSHIP DEVELOPMENT, AIG

positions, lead change, and achieve impact. One female executive we interviewed said, "As women, we feel like we are on the outside. We need to reframe the situation to see ourselves on the inside."

LIMITING BELIEFS That Weaken Our Access

The systemic challenges mentioned above make creating an infrastructure of support and reinforcement an ongoing necessity. Putting that idea into action, however, starts within each of us. We can begin by recognizing and addressing patterns of thinking that make it more difficult for us to access opportunities.

"One sponsor is all I need."

"I'll wait my turn."

"I should not ask for help."

"One sponsor is all I need"

True sponsorship, according to Sylvia Ann Hewlett, is not "sideline cheer-leaders" but "center-ring champions."[3] Linda's clearest miscalculation was rely-ing on a single sponsor. She was told by Ed that she would be elevated to partner without question. He was the leader on the firm's largest client; he would be retiring "soon"; and he had chosen her to replace him. But that never came to pass. Linda funneled her effort and trust into one relationship and it backfired. Her playbook had only ONE play. Trust and loyalty are important attributes, but they can leave you exposed and without support. It's far better to have several sponsors and advocates who compose your scaffolding of support—they will provide multiple perspectives and opinions. This is espe-cially important if you know one of your sponsors is exiting the company. In Linda's case, she found out after the fact that Ed was too busy managing the details of his impending retirement to lobby on her behalf. Even more, as a lame duck, he didn't have the political capital to deliver on his big promise.

We coach women to be aware that sponsors have goals and priorities of their own, and sometimes they simply don't align with ours in the moment. Ed was Linda's direct supervisor, so he was well placed to help her succeed. But it's even better to have additional sponsors and supporters at the highest levels across an organization.

"I'll wait my turn"

Linda believed that her time was coming. She worked hard, followed Ed's lead, and put in her time while waiting to make partner. She never made her desires widely known or asserted her intentions. This exemplifies a dual dynamic that we encounter frequently in our coaching work.

First, many female executives don't want to be perceived as overly ambitious—or "pushy"—so we wait politely for our big break instead of actively lobbying for support. Despite the impact of equality provisions such as Title IX, research shows that many girls are socialized at home and in school to be nice—nicer than boys. A study by Diane Reay, professor of education at the University of Cambridge, discovered that teachers and other authority figures in the classroom at one time discouraged assertive behavior in girls but reinforced it in boys. Reay says that the different ways teachers treated each gender at the time supported the idea that bad behavior in a girl should be considered a "character defect," whereas in boys it is to be viewed as "a desire to assert themselves."[4] Many of us still carry this perception with us to work.

The second dynamic at play here is risk aversion. Although some women are far more willing to take risks than others, research supports the idea that women may indeed be more risk averse than men in professional settings, perhaps because we have less leadership tenure and fewer role models.[5] However, when you build the right scaffolding, it provides the support you need to be bold and assertive. At Linda's next firm, she made it perfectly apparent—in words, deeds, and accomplishments—that her primary career objective was to become a partner and that any other path was not a part of her plan.

"I should not ask for help"

Asking for help (mentorship, sponsorship, and so on) is not in every woman's wheelhouse, and yet we do it in our personal lives regularly. Who is the best dentist? Where should my children go to school? What are the best neighborhoods in which to live? We are accustomed to multitasking and making things happen in other parts of our lives, but asking for help in our professional lives can make us feel exposed or weak.

Interestingly, men don't seem to share this particular hang-up. Although stereotypically they don't like stopping for directions on the street, they have no qualms about asking each other for professional support, favors, and other assistance on the job. In our interviews, dozens of women and men remarked that "men have each other's backs" and routinely engage in "quid pro quo deals" to help each other succeed. Men ask each other for help because they know that it goes both ways—when they ask for help, they will eventually offer support in return.

The pertinent idea here is that asking is a sign of strength rather than weakness. Ask for help from the people in your support scaffolding. When you ask for support, you are proposing a deal that will benefit both parties.

Questions for Reflection

➡ What steps could you take to turn a mentor into a sponsor?

➡ What are you doing to create strategic alignments with others?

➡ How are you preparing to take career risks? Do you have the support you need?

STRATEGIES to Build Your Scaffolding

Kay had a clear goal: "I know that I eventually want one of the top jobs."

After a while, she mustered the courage to tell her mentor about her goal. He reassured her that he thought she had what it took to take on a senior-level role. "Those jobs are hard to get," he said. "You will need broad support and sponsorship. You'd better start working on that now."

Kay was known as someone who was creative, could solve problems, and could get things done. However, she needed to raise her profile internally. So she got to work. She volunteered to help a senior leader in another department plan to execute a large annual client conference. She asked her mentor to nominate her to be on a division-wide committee. She spent time with colleagues across the division. She continued to do excellent work and shared credit with others.

Slowly but surely, Kay built sponsorship and support across the company. She created trusting relationships before they were needed.

A couple of years later, when it came time for a senior-level job to be filled, Kay had colleagues and sponsors who spoke up for her and supported her. She reached her career goal of having a seat at the leadership table.

There are some key lessons here. First, building support and sponsorship takes focus. You must be intentional about reaching out beyond the group of people who already support you. Second, your relationships must be authentic and reciprocal. Focusing only on yourself never works and can backfire. Finally, building sponsorship takes time. Look at it this way: You are building trust-based relationships that will last decades. You can't rush it.

STRATEGIES to Build Your Scaffolding

1. Create a personal board of directors.
2. Manage your mentor/sponsor mix.
3. Find an agent, truth teller, and personal supporter.
4. Work your scaffolding.

1. Create a personal board of directors

As we saw with Linda, one advocate is never enough, even if that person is a senior-level sponsor. We coach women to work their relationship maps and cultivate multiple advocates, up and down their career scaffolding, at various levels of the organization. Start your scaffolding with a small, manageable number of advocates and add additional supporters over time.

A compatible way to bring this idea to life is by building what we call a *personal board of directors*. Creating this board takes the pressure off when a big fish (like Ed) is unable or unwilling to help. It's yet another way to establish support and buy-in and avail yourself of advice and counsel, which our interviews highlighted as a crucial part of achieving influence.

This board is a group of people whom you go to for support and advice on advancing your career. Ideally, they are individuals who have a strong personal and professional interest in seeing you succeed. While there is no real board table and no official meetings, these handpicked advocates offer you access to a wider range of ideas, contacts, and support. They also understand you—your strengths as a leader and your gaps in terms of skills, knowledge, and opportunities.

Finally, creating a personal board of directors will give you the confidence you need to drive change and sell disruptive ideas. As we saw with Kay, the effort it takes to create strategic support scaffolding pays off, dramatically improving your odds of success.

Think about the people who can guide you, help you, and challenge you. Put their names in the chairs in Figure 7 and assemble a group that can help you navigate your career. Your larger scaffolding will grow from your personal board

FIGURE 7   Your Personal Board of Directors

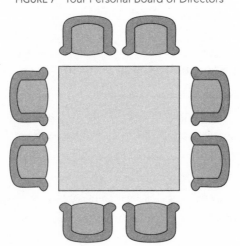

of directors. For the rest of this chapter, we'll take a closer look at the people in these chairs and how they make up your scaffolding.

2. Manage your mentor/sponsor mix

While both mentors and sponsors are critical toeholds in your scaffolding, each group has its own distinct utility. It's likely that you understand that a mentor is a role model—a coach who empowers, educates, and inspires you. He or she offers advice, experience-based strategies, intelligence, and veteran insights. Sponsors, on the other hand, provide not just advice but also access to opportunities. In other words, sponsors *pull you up* higher in the organization.

This difference is critical because women are "over-mentored, and under-sponsored."[6] In an article published in the *Harvard Business Review*, noted researchers from INSEAD and Catalyst showed that men in one study were promoted and paid more than female colleagues who had the same education and experience, even though more of the women reported having mentors.[7] What was happening here? The men had sponsors to help them move up into higher-level jobs. The same principle holds true for men and women: those who find sponsors have significantly more success in breaking into the higher levels of a company.

The rub is that effective, high-level sponsors are far harder to find than mentors. The best piece of advice we offer women to help them find sponsors is this: it's a reciprocal relationship. When you find the senior executive who is ideally aligned to help you move ahead, determine how you can help him or her by being a strategic ally.[8] In Sylvia Ann Hewlett's book *Forget a Mentor, Find a Sponsor*, she suggests that you should meet all of your sponsor's deadlines, generate outstanding results, and generally make your sponsor look good. You should also be fluent in sharing your accomplishments so your sponsor can recite them to others.[9]

Mentors are important (particularly when we are starting out in business), but sponsors serve to strengthen our scaffolding and add the type of support that we need to access opportunities that would otherwise be beyond our reach.

3. Find an agent, truth teller, and personal supporter

Mentors and sponsors are critical supporters in your scaffolding, but there are others to consider.

The agent. One of our clients, Lynn, told us something her new boss shared with her during her recent performance review. Her boss had just traveled to a conference with one of Lynn's direct reports, Glenn. During the flight, she asked him straight out, "So, what kind of leader is Lynn?" Glenn gushed, saying, "Oh, I've never had a better boss. She's great at developing our team, and she really cares about us and our work…and she's already working to implement your agenda for you."

Lynn told us, "I couldn't have prompted him to say nicer things about me." And she didn't need to prompt him. Glenn was one of Lynn's agents. Agents are the colleagues you are allied with at all levels of the organization. They appreciate you and trust you enough to vouch for you and promote you to peers. Agents are a positive by-product of all the relationships that you cultivate across your network. Agents don't require as much effort as sponsors; they simply require nurturing, as in any solid relationship. Your very best agents (we call them

---

Who Needs an Agent?

One of us has a friend whose son worked night and day for months to secure a tryout with the Carolina Panthers. He chose not to get a sports agent, but he was good enough to get a tryout. After a grueling full day in front of the coaches, he was selected to join the spring training camp for the final round of tryouts. It was showtime. When he arrived at camp, the coaches handed him an encyclopedia-size playbook. He had twenty-four hours to memorize all the plays. Later, he was in the hotel room he shared with a prospective teammate. He stayed up and studied all night, whereas his roommate sat back and played *Madden Mobile* on his phone, not so much as glancing at the playbook. Why? His agent got him the plays in advance. He already knew them.

It's the same in organizations. Agents find ways to help you succeed.

super agents) proactively look for opportunities to help you out by giving you important company intelligence and mentioning your name strategically in conversations.

The truth teller. Truth tellers are exactly what they sound like: the trusted allies who tell it like it is. They give you the unvarnished truth and say things to your face that no one else will. They are the ones who look you in the eye when you are up for a promotion and tell you, "If you don't work on your leadership skills you will never move up." Or, after a crucial presentation, "It went okay, but next time make eye contact and speak slowly." We may not always want to hear it, but the truth teller can jolt us back to reality.

Kay had a truth teller who saved her skin during the marketing reorganization. She was busy building her scaffolding, yet there was a mounting insurrection underfoot. A group of marketing associates feared losing their jobs in the reorganization, and they launched a negative campaign against Kay. Fortunately, she had a truth teller to confide exactly what was happening and why. Until then, Kay had no idea her plans were upsetting a vital cohort. In truth, their jobs were safe, but Kay had not communicated her intentions sufficiently, and her truth teller told her as much. Kay sprang to action, met with the naysayers, and put out the fire.

Having at least one truth teller as an advocate may seem like a no-brainer, but it's not always the case. As they say, "the truth hurts," and many of us don't want to hear it. Having the humility to listen to our trusted allies is one sure way to keep our scaffolding strong.

The personal supporter. Hardly a day passes in which we don't talk to a female executive who's feeling stretched to the limit trying to balance a high-demand job with her family life and personal commitments. There's always a crisis, either at home or at work. Even when everything is going well, fatigue can set in and throw us for a loop. We call this pitfall *the stress of success.*

One of the best ways to manage the stress of success is to remember to count friends and family as part of your support network. Whether it's a spouse, sibling, or close friend, we all need people in our scaffolding who are *always* on our side, looking out for us no matter what.

4. Work your scaffolding

Once you've created your scaffolding, you need to use it or lose it. Here are three ways to use your scaffolding effectively.

Access. The best use of your scaffolding is to create access not only to opportunities but also to top decision makers with whom you would otherwise not cross paths. Each level of support offers yet another step up. If you are working to sell an idea, begin with your foundation of supporters and work up from there. If one path is not helpful, try another side of your scaffolding. It's a lattice—interwoven and multisided. Being surrounded by support affords numerous options to access the highest levels of leadership. When Kay was making her case to reassign marketing personnel currently reporting to C-suite executives, she needed to tap more than one senior-level advocate to get buy-in.

Trusted allies. Cultivating professional relationships that are based on mutual trust accrues benefits that can never be discounted. All of us need professional allies in order to achieve success, but the supporters we surround ourselves with in our scaffolding should be those whom we trust enough to stand up for us in the best and worst of times. These particular allies mean more to us not only because they are steadfast but also because we've invested so much time and effort in earning their trust and support. Simply knowing they are there makes us (and our scaffolding) far stronger.

Acceleration. The initial effort you dedicate to constructing scaffolding enables you to bypass the politically charged, time-consuming task of lobbying for support every time you need to get something new accomplished. Yes, you will always need to make a cogent case for yourself and your ideas, but scaffolding that is assembled properly is adjustable, enduring, and reusable.

*   *   *

The final thing to remember about creating your scaffolding is that its multi-sided nature means that reciprocation is self-reinforcing. Paying it forward to support other colleagues strengthens your scaffolding as well as theirs. Similarly, your scaffolding is a primary component of the Influence Effect because the multiple levels of support and the safety afforded by solid scaffolding provide you with the confidence, in yourself and your career, to take chances on opportunities that you would otherwise feel too exposed to try.

Executive Summary

- Scaffolding is the lattice of support that we put into place around ourselves.
- Scaffolding gives us the confidence to think bigger and take chances. It provides us with access to opportunities and top leadership.
- Relying on a single sponsor or going it alone, as opposed to creating layers of support, leaves us at risk and exposed.
- We need to cultivate sponsors strategically and carefully manage our mentor/sponsor mix.
- Agents, truth tellers, and personal supporters are critical layers in strong scaffolding.
- Our scaffolding is strengthened when we reciprocate and support other colleagues in our network.

PART TWO

PRACTICE
The Big Five
Strategies

PREPARE
to Influence

PRACTICE:
The Big Five
Strategies

INFLUENCE
in Action

4

The Power of the Informal

*Bring people with positive energy into your inner
circle. If those around you are enthusiastic, authentic,
and generous, you will be, too.*

—ROB CROSS AND ROBERT J. THOMAS

*Anna had big plans to grow her department in 2016. The prior year was a clear
success, and she and her sales team closed more deals than ever before. It was
considered a coup to bring in new business when much of the sector—customer
service staffing—was losing out to cheaper global competitors and the remaining domestic jobs were being slashed and replaced by automation. Anna's team
outperformed expectations for two reasons. First, she steered their efforts toward
organizations that relied on U.S. government contracts for their livelihood.
These were businesses that had a vested interest in keeping their call centers
in the United States. Second, Anna created a service delivery system that brought
their costs for the call centers down 10 percent, and she could pass that savings
along to clients to help close deals.*

*With her system working so well, Anna put together a plan to roll the process
out across the organization and expand her team. Her plan called for a re-
structuring that she believed would lower their costs in the first eighteen*

months, but it required hiring several new midlevel managers. With enthusi-
astic approval from her manager, she presented the idea to the operating com-
mittee. Two meetings later, she secured tacit approval, as well as a nod from
the chief financial officer (CFO) that the funding would be earmarked for
her department in the next fiscal year's budget.

That was good enough for Anna. She celebrated with her team and made the
initial preparations for the expansion. She began identifying new staff mem-
bers and thinking about the change management effort. Two months later,
the budget documents were released. To Anna's shock, her 2016 budget was
essentially flat—no spending increase. Instead, the excess funds were flowing
in another direction, to a different department.

Anna was blindsided. She had not remained in contact with the CFO, and she
had taken too much for granted. What she didn't know at the time was that an-
other executive had gone to the CFO after her pitch meeting. He had an alternate
plan and made a play to secure the funding. After that, he spent the next couple of
months selling his idea behind the scenes. He had taken various managers to
lunch, and he walked up to the executive floor regularly to socialize before work.

Anna never really had a chance. She was a high performer and her plan was
smart and well conceived. The problem? She skipped the critical steps that occur
informally. Her colleague went the extra yard to get to know the decision makers
personally. He built relationships. He dedicated the time and effort to earn their
confidence and establish personal trust. He worked behind the scenes to create
an informal coalition of support. Anna never thought to do any of that. She
thought the formal process was all there was. To use our opening surfing metaphor, Anna caught the initial curls, but her colleague rode the entire wave.

THE UNWRITTEN RULE: Leverage
the Power of the Informal

We explored professional relationships and formal connections in the previous
chapter. Here, we'll examine a complementary but lesser-known element of influence that some of us still overlook: the power of the informal.

Informal power can be achieved in at least two ways: casual office interactions and social networks. Casual interactions occur during hours spent with colleagues on the clock, inside the office and out, when the focus is loose and off the cuff. Informal interactions happen as we stop to shoot the breeze before and after meetings, before and after work, at lunch, and at company activities such as dinners or events. Social networks are groups of colleagues who choose to spend some of their leisure time together outside the workplace, engaging in shared interests and activities, such as sporting events or the arts.

Regardless of the venue or activity, the power of the informal is an important way that we get to know and trust our colleagues—and how they get to know and trust us. It's how numerous deals are done and promotions are sealed. As Anna learned, it is also how many decisions are made. Informal interactions allow us to talk candidly, reinforce our key points, use humor, and trade favors in a way that would never work as part of a formal interaction or in an official setting.

The higher up we are in an organization, the more important informal interactions become. Yet we, as women, engage informally less often than men

---

What Our Interviews with Men Revealed

"Men work informally, outside formal settings, oftentimes more effectively than women. They know how the system works from being 'in charge' longer."

—W. FLETCHER WRIGHT, FORMER SOUTHEAST MANAGING PARTNER, DELOITTE

"Women don't have 'the meeting before the meeting' in the way that men do. And I'm not just talking about counting votes. We're listening, presenting facts, persuading and problem solving."

—MALE EXECUTIVE, PROFESSIONAL SERVICES FIRM

"Men rely on bars and sports and other social settings to win influence informally and curry favor in ways that women can't or don't."

—MIKE CLEMENT, MANAGING DIRECTOR, STRAIT INSIGHTS

because we face more unique challenges in pulling these nuanced relationships off. Debra Plousha Moore, system chief of staff at Carolinas HealthCare System, explained, "When women participate in political maneuvering, it looks more obvious because we are not part of the majority group. It can often seem less natural and more contrived. Men teach men how to politic. Women generally do not teach each other this important art."

It therefore becomes harder for women to make these informal connections.

For the most part, the women we interviewed agreed with the sentiments presented in the previous box. On the one hand, they told us that their ability to connect with colleagues and navigate in groups was *at least* as important to their career success as how they perform in their roles. On the other hand, they cited home or life priorities and "male-only" after-work activities as a few of the reasons they put informal interactions on the back burner.

LIMITING BELIEFS That Check Our Informal Power

We have found that small adjustments in thinking can empower women to unlock the power of informal interactions. With that in mind, let's look at three ways to re-imagine common scenarios to tilt the results in our favor.

"I have no time for networking."

"Nothing important happens at these things."

"I don't get invited."

"I have no time for networking"

Time constraints are the most common reason women cite for ditching dinner with colleagues or skipping other social events. (We can relate!) There are just twenty-four hours in a day, and we all need to make choices based on our values and circumstances. Because of that, it's important for us to maximize the time we *can* dedicate to building relationships. Whether after hours or during business hours, we tell women that creating informal connections is just another part of their job, particularly as they rise higher in the organization. Even if you are tight on time or simply disdain "networking," there are simple tactics to help you make the most of your effort:

- Forget about "networking"; this is about truly connecting.
- Focus on strategic relationship building as opposed to mindless "working the room."
- Consider your personal style and decide which way of connecting with people feels most natural to you. Put together a plan based on that.
- Connect in a way that suits your lifestyle—meet over a meal or coffee or at an industry event.
- Bake it into your schedule by setting time aside. We have clients who color-code their calendars to make sure they dedicate time to making connections. Others create lists or use simple Excel spreadsheets. One client goes through half her alphabet of contacts every six months to make sure she connects with each person.
- Just do it—don't opt out.

"Nothing important happens at these things"

Sometimes, *nothing important happens at these things*…and that's an excellent reason to be there. During a typical, fully packed day of conference calls and meetings, there's little or no unscheduled time, unscripted conversations, or easy access to colleagues from across the organization.

Unscheduled time (during a company party, for instance) allows you to create your own agenda. Let's say that you were in a meeting with a colleague last week and you need some additional information. Instead of scheduling formal time to reconnect, catching the colleague for a few minutes in between calendar commitments provides a chance to get some questions answered. Or perhaps you need buy-in from a sales director who's always out on the road. Unscheduled time together offers an opportunity to plant a seed or test an idea.

Unscripted conversations that occur off the clock can be as refreshing as they are enlightening. People let their hair down in informal settings. Nobody's really loving the new branding campaign? You may hear about it walking over to the train together after work. Sometimes even the most introverted colleagues open up about themselves. They may tell you something about their personal circumstances that explains their demeanor at work. Regardless of the content, unscripted conversations help us get to know people better and cement our understanding of what's really going on in the office.

If nothing else, informal social settings can be an excellent equalizer. An event at which top-level executives, staffers, and everyone else munches on the same cocktail olives is an open opportunity to meet new people and hear what they have to say.

"I don't get invited"

Our client Cara told us this was her rationale for leaving company events and board meetings early. Then, after a particular quarterly sales conference, the light went on in her head. At the time, the senior staff on the international marketing team was exiting the big ballroom together, and most of them were walking out to have dinner as a group. Cara wasn't invited. She was about to catch a cab and head home to check e-mails and get some work done before sending the babysitter home. As she got into a cab, one of the guys called out to her and said, "Cara, aren't you coming?" She replied, "Oh, I wasn't invited." They all laughed, and the male colleague said, "Get out of that cab. Come on, go with us." She did. Cara had a drink and appetizers and headed home, but she gained a realization: "Nobody really gets invited. Most men don't formally invite each other," she said, laughing. "They just go... everyone just goes!"

Are there times when just a few people need to go out together to talk about a specific issue or close a private deal? Sure. But more often than not, you don't really need a reason to join the group for drinks and dinner. This is how people decompress, talk about what they're working on, and get to know each other. No invitation needed.

There are several variations on the "I wasn't invited" theme. Sometimes it sounds like, "I do not have anything to talk to them about anyway" or "I really cannot relate to them because they are so much older (or have different interests). What could we possibly have in common?" You insert the reason! One of the more common rationales we hear is, "I do not play golf."

Many of the women we coach say that their golf game (or lack thereof) feels like a legitimate barrier to informal networking. And it's no wonder. Although only 20 percent of golfers are women, a whopping 90 percent of Fortune 500 CEOs play golf, and 80 percent of executives say playing golf enables them to establish new business relationships.[1] But, to be clear, it is not golf per se that's the issue. Men seldom wait to be invited. And yes, opportunities may occur more naturally for them, but we need to look for ways to opt in instead of looking for excuses to opt out.

Teresa Tanner, executive vice president and chief administrative officer at Fifth Third Bank, told us why this ideal can be a challenge for women: "From a politics standpoint, building relationships is important and yet, depending upon the values and activities shared among leaders of the organization (whether that is charity work, sports, theater), we may not have the same volume of opportunities [as men] to build trust, build relationships, and network informally."

Many of the men we interviewed concurred with Teresa's assessment. This story from a male executive in our study sums up the situation:

> *I was walking through the downstairs grill at a private club in town. I've been there a few times, but I'm not a member. If you're a stranger, you don't quite know how to fit in. I watched the men who dominate that network. They're laid back and they make funny remarks to each other. When I settled in, I looked like I belonged, even though I was not sure about some of the*

remarks and funny lines. Imagine a woman who is put into this environ-
ment. She would have to put much more energy into finding a way to fit in,
because she is still such a rarity. If she doesn't figure out the landscape, she
will stand out even more. She will spend a tremendous amount of energy
simply "fitting in."

All the energy we must expend trying to fit in on the golf course, in the club grillroom, and even in the boardroom makes informal networking more of a challenge for us, but that doesn't mean we should opt out. Women need to think of new solutions to this old problem—and that does not mean we need to learn golf. Unless, of course, we *want* to play golf.

One company we work with found a way to change up their annual golf event in a way that works for everyone. The rules are that all employees attend. The organizers go to great lengths to make the day about team building as opposed to an actual golf game. The men and the women who like golf can choose from a few different interactive rounds, like best ball or a round robin. Men and women who don't play can take lessons, try tennis, or simply relax with a leisurely hike or another resort activity. Everyone is invited. More importantly, however, it is not about being engaged in an activity; it is about creating opportunities for interpersonal connections to occur.

Questions for Reflection

➡ What is holding you back? What opportunities could you take advantage of to interact informally?

➡ What role models do you have when it comes to connecting informally? Which of their techniques could you emulate?

➡ How can you make informal networking a part of your job?

STRATEGIES for Using the
Power of the Informal

Increasingly, leadership today is defined not just by how many hours you spend at your computer, but your ability to connect to others.

—CAROL BARTZ, FORMER YAHOO CEO[2]

When we think about the power of the informal, there is one female leader, Maggie, whom we consider to be a role model. She is a master at the art of relationships, and this talent has served her well. She is recognized for a lengthy and successful stint as the chief executive of a nationally known company. She has also held other well-known positions, and she currently sits on several corporate boards. She has done all of this while raising a son and enjoying a rich social life filled with deep relationships.

We have seen Maggie in action and she is best in class. We recall one instance when Maggie was starting in a new position as the chief executive of a huge national nonprofit organization. Because her previous job had been a high-profile role in big business, her move to the nonprofit role rubbed many of the leaders at her new organization the wrong way. To make matters worse, there was some bad history between Maggie's former employer and the nonprofit because of legislation that Maggie's former organization lobbied hard for and the nonprofit vigorously opposed. As a result, a small but critical segment of leaders at the nonprofit were outwardly hostile toward Maggie in her first weeks on the job.

About a week into Maggie's appointment, two of us ran into an old colleague, Jim, who was a board member from the nonprofit. He was also a big donor and an influential figure at the organization. After the requisite small talk, the subject of Maggie came up, and Jim said, "I am not a fan. I was opposed to her appointment and I will never be able to work with her." We urged him to give Maggie a chance, but he insisted that there was "no way" she would win him over.

Knowing Maggie as we did, we smiled and told Jim we hoped he would ultimately reconsider. Sure enough, nine months later, we saw Jim, and Maggie had managed to get him on her team. Jim told us what happened.

He and Maggie both attended the first board meeting, where introductions were made. After the meeting, Maggie stopped him to mention a friend they had in common. She shook his hand and left it at that. The next time he saw her, she was in an elevator on her way to a meeting. The elevator door opened to Jim's floor, but it wasn't Maggie's destination. She got off anyway and walked right over to Jim to ask his advice about a piece of business. The third time she saw him, it was at a fund-raiser. She went right up to him, shook his hand, and asked if they could meet for coffee. Before Jim even knew it, they had met for coffee and had plans to take their mutual friend out to dinner together.

Maggie won Jim over because she is extremely good at connecting with people. She does her homework, finds common ground, uses her time wisely, and sincerely cares about others. She works hard to build trust. In short, she is an expert at the power of the informal.

STRATEGIES for Using the Power of the Informal

1. Make meaningless time meaningful.
2. Hold the meeting before the meeting.
3. Understand the informal norms.
4. Do it your way.
5. Talk the talk.

1. Make meaningless time meaningful

Women are master planners, and we are excellent at execution. This tells us that we have ample opportunity to make the most of informal interactions simply by being strategic. This is particularly true for women to whom social engagement does not come naturally. We tell the women we coach to think of it this way: make your meaningless time more meaningful. In other words, maximize your time and never underestimate how far this investment will take you. Try it for a predetermined period of time and watch for the dividends.

Here's how to begin.

Set small goals. When you make up your mind to spend an hour at a cocktail party after work, decide in advance what you'll accomplish. *Have an innovative idea you need to put to the test?* Identify three savvy colleagues and talk them through your plan. *Need to make more high-level connections?* Identify a few executives and introduce yourself. Regardless of what you need to achieve, plan ahead and use your informal time wisely.

Make networking work for you. One of us is friendly with an executive who runs a successful commercial real estate firm in Washington, DC. Her job is high touch, and she knows everyone inside the Beltway. And yet, she's also the single mother of a six-year-old and she loves to be home to tuck in her daughter. How does she keep all those plates spinning? She allows herself one night during the workweek to be out late. It might be a client dinner or a DC networking event. A single evening each week might not seem like a lot, she admits, but it adds up quickly. She maximizes her time and sticks to a plan that suits her life. All of us can do that. Whether you decide to arrive at work early twice a week for some face time, or you have lunch with colleagues every third Friday, identify what works for you and follow through. No excuses!

Take a walk. We know a savvy publishing executive who arrives early to the office each morning and walks around the floors of the building. Sometimes she has an agenda, other times she simply stops to chat with whoever's milling around. She always catches somebody and finds out what's going on. It's her early warning system. If she's proposing a new book series at the following week's meeting, she gets the early feedback and she's more prepared for her presentation.

Put your phone down. It's not only millennials who can't take their eyes away from their smartphones; screens rob all of us of precious face-to-face interactions. This is an easy one if you set your mind to it: stop hiding behind your phone. Talk to people before the meeting starts, on your way to lunch, on the stairs, and in the elevator. Simply looking people in the eye when you're talking with them will help you make that crucial connection.

2. Hold the meeting before the meeting

We heard from men and women alike that female executives are very efficient. We come to meetings on time. We leave when the last agenda item is completed. Then we rush to the next commitment, or head back to our offices to put out fires. But let's think for a minute about our male colleagues. Men are more likely to come early, get a good seat, and chat with colleagues. They stick around after the meeting to close off the discussion and talk informally about the other issues on their minds.

"Men talk to everyone before the meeting starts to take the temperature in the room," Monika Machon, a former financial services executive, told us. "They don't even think about it, it's just something they do, like breathing."

These interactions occur in the days, hours, or minutes prior to a meeting or decision. The conversations are informal and occur in passing: in the hallway, in the elevator, or on the walk to the train. This "meeting before the meeting" is where the real work happens, and how key issues are resolved.

This is one of the most important strategies we teach women: if we wait until the meeting starts to express our views, it's already too late. Well before a decision is to be made, we should test our perspective with colleagues and build consensus. Far from being a mere schmooze-fest, the time before and after a meeting is a chance to connect with colleagues informally, share your ideas, and gain their trust. Anna, from our earlier story, learned this lesson too late. She was sure she had sold her plan to the executive team, until her colleague worked behind the scenes to close his own deal.

Karen Dahut, executive vice president at Booz Allen Hamilton, put it this way: "Always come to meetings already knowing where everyone stands on an issue. If you don't, then you aren't in the best position possible to influence them."

Establishing a bond with people prior to the meeting can also help you feel confident. That confidence makes it easier to participate and engage in the discussion. In the same way that getting to know the room in advance of a speech helps individuals become acclimated to the space, connecting with people informally creates a sense of familiarity.

3. Understand the informal norms

Is your workplace a coffee culture, or do people head to the bar for a beer after work? Informal rituals are important to understand because they make professional networking easier to accomplish. There's no need to get a lunch on the calendar if you know the executive vice president will be in line at Starbucks every morning at eight o'clock. Many organizations have birthday lunches, whereas others have Monday-morning bagels. Regardless of the specifics, seize opportunities to make connections and let other people get to know you.

Similarly, examine the cross-silo *social networks* that underlie your organization. Does the tech-savvy set all sit together at staff meetings and text each other the whole time? Do the young moms meet for coffee on Mondays? Even if you don't fit within any of the social networks yourself, simply knowing who does can tell you who's closely connected to whom. This applies to the social networking *tools* that people use as well. Knowing how people communicate allows you to reach out to them in ways that best suit them.

4. Do it your way

Informal networking and socializing is never a one-size-fits-all proposition. In fact, it can make you miserable unless you do it in a manner that suits your style. Here's what we suggest.

Suit yourself. Don't bother learning to play tennis if that's not your thing. Decide what you like—opera, ballgames, trendy eateries—and invite a few colleagues along for the fun. Doing something that you enjoy and are good at not only makes you happy, it also makes you more comfortable and puts you in charge in a way that can change how people perceive you.

Use the group dynamic. If you are an introvert, you don't need to go it alone. Meet a few work friends and head to the company picnic with them. It's fine to work the room in pairs. The same goes for informal socializing. It doesn't need to be a one-on-one event. Getting a group together to have drinks or dinner makes it easier to talk to someone you don't know.

Have people into your home. We know many women who prefer to invite colleagues and their spouses or partners over to their home instead of meeting together solo or going out to dinner together. Most of us are more comfortable on our own turf. In addition, bringing people to your home helps them get to know you better.

Find a women's network. A few years ago, one of our coaching clients who works at a bank ran into a colleague on her way into the office. She hadn't seen him in a while and he looked tan and relaxed. She said, "So, what have you been up to?" He told her he had just gotten back from a weeklong fishing trip in Panama. She smiled and responded, "Oh, wow, did you take your two sons?" "Oh, no. It was a big group of guys from the bank. We had a blast."

At first, the conversation made her feel uneasy. She was thinking about how many deals got closed during that trip and how many sponsorship relationships were cemented. But then, gradually, an entirely different thought crossed her mind: what a great idea!

She doesn't like to fish, but she loves going to wine tastings. For the past three years she's gone to a different wine region for a weekend away each year with her friends from work. They spend the time hiking, biking, and sampling great wine. And guess what? *They have a blast.*

5. Talk the talk

It's not rocket science, but there's an art to the informal. You will not be a master at it at first, but keep practicing by using these tips:

- Keep the talk light. Informal networking should be casual and social. Your conversation needs a relevant point, but it need not be uptight, structured, or overly serious. (Yes, this means avoiding politics and religion.)
- Give something to get something. People love to learn something new and important. Think about what you can tell them to help them understand the context of a situation, for instance, or explain why a controversial decision was made. After that, they'll be more willing to engage with you and tell you what's on their mind.
- Don't overshare. Getting too personal or baring your soul makes people uncomfortable. Likewise, sharing company secrets destroys trust and gets you into trouble. In other words, keep informal networking…informal. It's fine to wing it, but remain within these smart, simple parameters.

* * *

Like the other strategies in this book, the power of the informal is something all of us can learn and practice. In time, it will become second nature. As one of your tools of influence, informal interactions will have bona fide benefits when mastered.

Many of the women we coach guard their free time and insist that they don't have the desire to get to know their colleagues on a more personal basis. Our philosophy has always been, *try it and see how it works for you*. Stop overrelying on e-mail and texting and get up and talk to people face to face. Engage, ask questions, and find out about them. When someone reaches out to you, go have lunch with him or her. If an old college roommate asks you to help her son with his job search, talk to him. Do favors and then ask for a favor in return.

Much of the advice in this chapter requires a leap of faith. How do we know it works? We've tried it ourselves. One of us, in particular, prides herself on

never saying no to a favor. She spends much of her time on relationship building. She sees the world through people and relationships. Life has taught her
that it all comes back to you when you need it. This approach to life can bring
you new business, support you in times of stress, create relationships that nurture you, and help you remain engaged in our fully connected world.

Give networking a shot. You'll love what happens.

Executive Summary

- Informal networking is just another part of our job, particularly as we rise higher in the organization.
- We don't need a formal agenda to join the group for coffee or dinner. This is how people decompress, talk about what they're working on, and get to know each other. No invitation is needed.
- All of the energy we expend trying to fit in—on the golf course, in the club grillroom, and even in the boardroom—makes informal relationship building more of a challenge for us.
- The "meeting before the meeting" is where the real work happens. If we wait until the meeting starts to express our views, it's already too late. We should test our perspectives with colleagues in advance and build consensus.
- Informal networking and socializing is never a one-size-fits-all affair. We need to find a way to make it suit our style.

5

Relationship Maps

*If you believe business is built on relationships,
make building them your business.*

—SCOTT STRATTON AND ALLISON KRAMER

Catherine was a wizard with numbers. She was a strategic thinker who was accustomed to being the brightest finance mind in the room. She attended a prestigious university and went on to Harvard Business School. In the first third of her career, Catherine worked at a small but elite private equity firm, where she made a name for herself using financial modeling to identify undervalued companies in the media and entertainment sector.

The firm where she worked was full of savvy individual contributors who thrived in the highly competitive, high-adrenaline culture. The bankers who delivered the most deals got promoted. Although Catherine generally came out looking great based on her brainpower, she wasn't gaining the recognition from the senior partners that she expected. In time, she decided to make the move to a company that could provide a clearer career path and the chance to run the finance side of a growing business.

With her résumé and Ivy League connections, Catherine had little difficulty moving into an executive finance role at a media conglomerate. Her job was managing the numbers for one of the organization's most visible business units. She worked closely with the chief operating officer and she reported directly to the CFO. Catherine had every reason to believe that she was the full package—smart, insightful, and hard working. Unfortunately, she had an Achilles' heel that trumped her strengths and eventually set her career back significantly.

Catherine worked hard and was very bright, but at times she acted in an arrogant manner—like she knew more than everyone else. She believed her strong performance would always be enough and she did not need anyone's support. As a result, her key connections never became strong relationships, much less solid allies or advocates.

The cracks became evident about a year into her tenure. The company was heading into a buying spree, picking up smaller players and integrating them into the portfolio. Catherine knew a great deal about buyouts from her private equity days, and she became a vocal critic of several deals that she felt sure were mistakes. She spent long nights reviewing every aspect of potential deals. When proposals she disliked came up for discussion, she invariably excoriated the deal sponsors and anyone on the team who supported them. When individuals disagreed with her perspective, she vocalized her dissent forcefully and publicly. One day she made the mistake of roundly disparaging a potential deal that had the implicit blessing of the CFO and CEO. After that, the CEO was no longer her supporter. Catherine's executive colleagues, seeing an opportunity, publicly turned against her. She came to realize just how alone and exposed she was.

When we met with Catherine a few months later, conditions had not improved, and she was feeling confused and isolated. We spoke to her colleagues as part of our coaching process, and the results couldn't have been clearer: her success in the past was heavily dependent on individual performance, whereas her current job required teamwork, the sharing of information, and the creation of a consensus.

Catherine had failed to understand a paramount tenet for success: you can't have influence without forging strategic, mutually beneficial relationships. We tell this unique story to make our point. We know Catherine is not every woman, but you must never underestimate the power of relationships and building trust with your colleagues. Rarely do we see a Catherine succeed.

THE UNWRITTEN RULE: Relationships Drive Influence

As women, we are naturally skilled relationship builders in our personal lives. All four of us are spouses, mothers, sisters, and friends, and we've spent what cumulatively amounts to many lifetimes supporting (and being supported by) our friends and families. Yet, as executive coaches, we see that we, as women, don't always bring that innate ability with us when we forge careers and drive our professional agendas.

In Catherine's case, she didn't recognize until it was too late how she was "landing on" her colleagues—that is, how they perceived her words and actions. She was not aware that her take-no-prisoners nature was destroying the few relationships she had managed to forge. As we rise through the ranks at work, all of us need to bring the full package forward, and that includes being cognizant of where we stand with colleagues. In our research, we found that women have a higher degree of difficulty, compared to male colleagues, in creating and sustaining a strong cadre of influential allies who will advance our ideas and boost our careers. In part, this is because men tap into the existing male network that has been built up over many generations. Another theory is that we, as women, don't prioritize connection time—we're busy balancing the competing demands of family and career. In addition, many women roundly disdain activities that fall under the banner of "office politics." Building coalitions and developing alliances can seem like dirty pool to some of us.

As we move into higher levels of leadership, it's important to think about key business relationships in a more strategic way. It requires doing your homework and getting to know your organization: Who are the influencers, the decision makers, the gatekeepers, and so on? Coalitions require connections, and relationship building, therefore, becomes a prerequisite for influence.

What Our Interviews Revealed

"Influence is about being aligned with the 'right' leaders. It may be more natural for men to align and connect because there are still more men in leadership positions."

—ALICIA ROSE, GLOBAL LEAD CLIENT SERVICE PARTNER FOR AMERICAN EXPRESS, DELOITTE & TOUCHE

"Women need to understand that influence is chiefly about understanding who the decision makers are and leveraging those relationships at work."

—DIRECTOR-LEVEL FEMALE EXECUTIVE, GLOBAL REAL ESTATE FIRM

"We need to forge relationships in order to get to know who decides, how they decide, and how to have influence over the decision."

—KATY HOLLISTER, MANAGING PARTNER, STRATEGY, GLOBAL TAX AND LEGAL, DELOITTE

One reason women neglect to make the right connections at the office may be related to gender dynamics. Linguistics and communications expert Deborah Tannen asserts that men and women make connections very differently. Women, she says, look for similarities between people, and they make connections by fostering common ground. Men focus on differences—in status or skills—and they connect by engaging with each other through good-natured banter and competition.[1] We believe our focus on common ground is a plus for women; however, we often fail to use it in our professional lives.

LIMITING BELIEFS: What's Holding You Back?

There's no doubt that fostering professional relationships requires a commitment to connecting with like-minded allies, supportive followers, executive sponsors, mentors, and many others. In our work, we help women with this critical endeavor, and we will mention some tricks of the trade that make it more manageable. First, there are several limiting beliefs and behaviors that hold us back from building the strategic relationships we need to succeed.

"Hard work is what matters most."

"I need to like (and trust) them . . . and be liked back."

"It's personal."

"Hard work is what matters most"

By all accounts, Catherine worked long hours and was a brilliant financial strategist. As we saw, that wasn't enough. In fact, Catherine was judged less on what she achieved than on what she failed to achieve. She hadn't cultivated professional relationships.

There are a couple of factors at play in this limiting belief. First, we know that the corporate world is not strictly egalitarian. Hard work gets us noticed early in our careers, but higher-order accomplishments—like followership and results—matter more as we move up the organizational food chain. A number of women put it succinctly in our interviews, including one C-suite executive at a nonprofit, who told us, "Women have seen that it is not always the most capable person who gets promoted. We need to take the time to look around and understand how decisions are really made, because it is not based on merit alone."

As we tell the women we coach, hard work is just the table stake. Once you have a seat at the table, success and influence stem from relationships and followership.

Similarly, working hard is not the same as working strategically. The projects that monopolize our attention are not necessarily the ones that offer the prestige and visibility of high-profile assignments. Being strategic is about knowing when to say yes and when to say no. A wise woman once told us not to check the same box twice. If you have already led that task force or served on that internal committee, then don't say yes again. If influence is the goal, then it is crucial to work strategically with a larger purpose in mind.

In short, working hard is necessary but not sufficient for achieving influence. Forging professional relationships and organizational alignments is the real "hard work" that needs to get done.

What got you here won't take you there![2]

What Our Research Told Us

"Women tend to keep their heads down and 'just work harder.'"
—MIKE RIZER, HEAD OF COMMUNITY RELATIONS, WELLS FARGO

"Women focus on doing the job. They believe others will align with them because it is the right thing to do. Men know they have to put together a marketing campaign around their idea or initiative."
—FEMALE EXECUTIVE, FINANCIAL SERVICES INDUSTRY

"I need to like (and trust) them . . . and be liked back"

Women take relationships seriously. As a result, we sometimes put conditions on professional interactions and make them more complicated than they need to be.

I need to like them. In one instance, a client told us she wasn't interested in meeting an influential colleague (and potential future sponsor) because *she wasn't sure she liked the colleague.* This is a common refrain. In our work, we see that women want to *like* people before they connect with them at corporate events, dinners, and off-sites. This type of unnecessary "friendship filter" leads to missed opportunities and lost chances to get to know the people who can help us succeed. The reality is that we may never really like the person who ends up being our strongest ally on a key project. More important than liking them is getting to know them and determining whether there is common ground from which to move forward.

I need to trust them. Another filter many of us use in office interactions is trust. We stay far away from the people we deem untrustworthy. Perhaps we think these individuals are "political" or we suspect that they don't have our best interests at heart. *News flash*: not trusting someone is an excellent reason to get to know him or her. Once you become acquainted, you might decide that the person is indeed trustworthy. If not, at least you've gained some insight into how he or she thinks and acts. In other words, knowledge is power. It is important to know whom you can trust, but it's even more important to manage relationships proactively. In our own careers, we have faced colleagues and bosses whom we did not trust. All of us need to navigate these dicey relationships, not fight them or ignore them.

I need them to like me. Just as we want to like the people we align with at work, we also want them to like us back. We want to be seen as *nice*, and it can keep us from achieving influence. Part of what sustains this limiting belief is the double bind that says women at work can be *liked* or they can be *competent*—but they can't be both. This age-old barrier is out there in full force. In our research, we found that the vast majority of men (65.9 percent) and women (81.9 percent) agree that women are still judged differently, and more harshly, than men when they use the tools of influence.

This double bind plays into three distinct dynamics that affect how we forge our professional relationships:

- *Women don't want to be perceived as phony.* Many women don't like "working the room" in meetings. We feel inauthentic when we scope out the people who can help us succeed professionally. The result? We avoid these situations entirely.
- *Women don't like to ask for help.* Research shows that women are less comfortable asking for what we want or need, including select assignments, sponsors, pay increases, and promotions.[3] We don't ask for these and other favors, in part, because we don't want to damage

our relationships or be seen as users. What does this mean for us? People do not know what we need and therefore cannot help us have the careers we desire.

- *Women don't trade favors.* Several of the women and men we interviewed said that they believe women are less comfortable than men when thinking about relationships as transactional in nature. Women, then, are less likely to engage in dealmaking that would benefit them because they don't want to be seen as calculating. How does that play out? We hold on to all our "frequent flyer miles" (favors owed to us) and never cash them in!

Clearly, we must gain respect and be taken seriously to achieve the type of influence we want. Although being liked certainly is helpful, it is just a small part of the influence equation.

"It's personal"

Many of us dislike sports metaphors and battle analogies in business. And yet, a number of men told us they internalize the idea that business is like a game. The metaphor helps them remain neutral—you win some, you lose some. They don't take criticism or professional slights personally. One chief operating officer told us, "Men realize that sometimes you lose the battle but you can still win the war." Another male executive put it like this: "Men beat each other up in a meeting and then go out and have a beer together. It's in our DNA and it's reinforced by our experiences growing up."

Women, however, told us that business relationships feel personal to them and they get "stuck in the moment" when situations go awry. Karen Dahut, executive vice president at Booz Allen Hamilton, told us about an experience from earlier in her career that's indicative of this limiting belief:

> I was in an executive committee meeting a while back and I put out some controversial points. I knew they would be controversial. We debated for a good while. I led the heated debate but eventually realized we could go no further, so I closed the conversation. But I thought about it for the entire weekend. I worried about

harming my [professional] relationships. I wondered what it would take to get them back on track. Then, on Monday, I saw some of my male colleagues and they greeted me as usual. I worried about it all weekend... and to them it was nothing!

Taking difficult professional interactions personally has a toll on women and makes it more difficult for us to manage relationships strategically and establish the type of influence we need to lead.

Questions for Reflection

➡ How are decisions made within your organization?

➡ What are the power dynamics?

➡ Who are the formal and informal influencers, and who makes the decisions?

➡ If the influencers and decision makers do not know you, what will you do to get on their radar?

STEPS for Making Relationships Strategic

You have to figure out the way decisions get made in the white space and who makes them. Influence and relationships always overlap.

—KATY HOLLISTER, MANAGING PARTNER, STRATEGY,
GLOBAL TAX AND LEGAL, DELOITTE

Sharon was thrilled and excited to move into a leadership role that was only two levels away from the executive team running the organization. But she was also extremely nervous. Her company was a large, diverse, suit-and-tie culture that was filled with high-caliber people. The field itself—management consulting—was notoriously competitive, and Sharon's firm was no exception.

Sharon had a lot of things going for her: She was excellent at her job and made a name for herself as a big-picture thinker. She was able to read the mood of a room and identify the underlying interpersonal dynamics. Yet her new role would not be without challenges: She needed to prove herself to her new boss, Larry, and his cadre of senior executive peers. And she also needed to get to know the CEO if she was going to succeed in her role and move up again soon. There were two women on the top tier of the company (alongside the CEO and three other men), and Sharon's ultimate goal was to leap two levels and join them.

We began coaching Sharon as soon as her promotion was finalized. She gave us a rundown on the firm and the entire senior management team, including nuanced insights into each person's personality and what she perceived to be his or her motivation. Sharon had done her homework. We talked to her about how she could carve a place for herself among the other leaders by focusing on building strategic relationships with her new peers, as well as the executive team.

She began by meeting weekly with Larry. The best thing she could do, she reasoned, was to interact with him in a positive way, continue to make a good impression, and succeed at her job overall. By delivering results and including him in her plans, she made him look good. Sharon had a talent for creating a halo effect around her close colleagues. It didn't take long for Larry to become a fan.

The culture at the firm was the same as it had been for decades—decentralized and social. Following Larry's counsel, Sharon planned a lunch with the CEO and started to interact with him whenever she had the chance—at meetings and occasionally over coffee. In time, and as Sharon's business continued to deliver strong results, she established trust with the CEO, who eventually became a strong advocate.

The five-member management team was a somewhat tougher nut to crack. To help her think through her strategy for building those relationships, Sharon pulled out a legal pad and mapped out the leadership team: their roles within the company, how they were aligned with each other, their relationship with the CEO, and some notes to herself about their business goals. It took some time, but she met with them, one by one, over a period of months and

*managed for the most part to win their tacit support. She looked for oppor-
tunities to interact with them and reinforce the initial connections she established. Eventually, it came down to two stubborn holdouts that Sharon felt
were less eager to support her—and were quite possibly willing to block her
next promotion.*

*Sharon took a proactive, long-term approach to the problem. First, she man-
aged to get herself placed on a project team that was extremely important to
one of the holdouts. She showed her support for his vested interests by moving
the project to the next level, and it went a long way toward cementing the relationship. That last individual? Well, Sharon was never able to get through to
him, and she struggles with the relationship even today.*

*Still, Sharon's efforts and her natural talent with people landed her a promo-
tion and a senior management assignment. About a year later, due to some
organizational changes and a retirement, Sharon was appointed to the executive team of the organization—her ultimate objective.*

There's a lot we can learn from Sharon. Her natural ability to forge relationships and bring people over to her side is worth examining. And it's also worth
noting that once Sharon reached her objective and received her seat on the
leadership team, several things changed for her, but one big thing remained the
same: she still needed to work as hard as ever to manage relationships.

STEPS for Making Relationships Strategic

1. Begin with the end in mind.
2. Draw a relationship map.
3. Examine the culture.
4. Establish common ground.
5. Take action!

1. Begin with the end in mind

In *The 7 Habits of Highly Successful People,* Stephen Covey says that beginning with the end in mind means maintaining "a clear vision of your desired direction and destination, and then flexing your proactive muscles to make things happen."[4]

Strategically managing office relationships begins with nurturing your vision, which we explored in chapter 2. Sharon's vision led directly to her spot on the executive team. Unlike many of us, she internalized where she wanted to go and cultivated the right relationships to get her there. Whether your goal is to sell a particular idea or land a new job, achieving it entails looking at relationships through two lenses: planning and focus.

Planning is a core part of building and maintaining the right professional relationships. It entails looking at all the things you want to achieve and isolating what's really important. After that, planning is about reviewing goals periodically, determining if you are on the right course, changing direction as needed, and knowing how to measure success. Having these steps in mind guides you as you decide how to network and who to engage for assistance.

Let's look at Sharon's situation:

Goal: Have a seat at the leadership table.

Why: To be able to have her voice impact the future of the firm.

Situation: Sharon had longevity at the firm with a successful track record. Her business was booming and she was given much of the credit for that success. She was a known people person. She sat two levels away from the leadership table.

Need: Build critical relationships in order to move up as circumstances allowed. Be at the top of the list for future leadership positions.

The focus phase is less straightforward. Focus is the link that connects planning and execution. In order to factor relationships into your strategic focus, you need to know the people and political dynamics of the organization and understand how the two overlap. (This is where Catherine went wrong: she had a plan, but she failed to factor in people and relationships.) The best way we know to connect these dots is to draw a relationship map.

2. Draw a relationship map

The primary tool we use to help women become role-model relationship builders is called a *relationship map*. Relationship maps are utilized most frequently in sales jobs to help salespeople close deals by mapping out influencers, decision makers, deal advocates, and deal blockers. Many times, sales organizations use complex software and lead generation databases to help people create the relationship maps they need.

For our purposes, the only prop required is a legal pad, a whiteboard, or a simple online chart you can create yourself—use whatever format is easiest for you to work with. Figure 8 contains some simple relationship map formats for you to consider that will help you visualize the work ahead of you.

FIGURE 8   Relationship Maps—Four Formats That Work

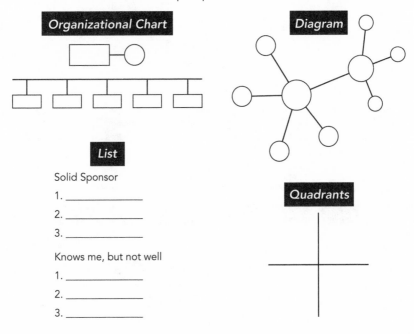

Relationship maps can help you achieve influence by creating a structure to accomplish three things:

Understand your network. A relationship map guides us to visualize our network of colleagues, as well as relevant outside parties and stakeholders, to identify the people who are in the best position to help us achieve our objectives.

Figure 9 shows Sharon's relationship map as it looked when she received her initial promotion. These were the teams that would ultimately decide her fate, and she was starting in a position of relative strength because she had strong connections with some of them already.

Sharon was operating two levels below the executive team. Her goal was to move up quickly and be the third woman appointed to the five-member team. In order to achieve that lofty objective, she identified the executive colleagues whom she would need to interact with. In some cases, she would simply need

FIGURE 9　Sharon—Her Relationship Map

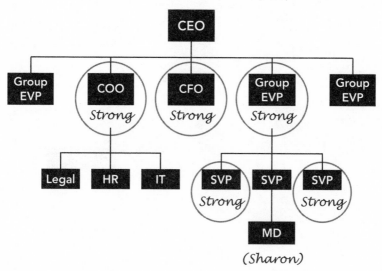

to become closely acquainted with the person; in others, she would need to win the person over to become an ally or a sponsor.

Map out meaningful connections. Relationship maps help us identify where people are positioned as part of an organizational hierarchy or influence network. They also help us understand whose opinion carries weight and who is closely connected to the main decision makers. As part of the mapping process, it is smart to consider how informal networks come into play and recognize that job titles do not always equal influence. It is important, as well, to construct your map with your professional objective in mind.

On Sharon's map, we see five direct reports to the CEO. Sharon had three of these individuals as sponsors already. An additional two were closely aligned with the CEO, and not strongly allied with Sharon. The CEO, who was new to the organization, did not know Sharon well and would not promote her without more "votes" for her from the others. She went to work based on that knowledge.

Enact a plan. Formulate an action plan by examining your relationship map and asking yourself these questions:

- Who do I need to get to know to achieve my objective? What's important to them? Sharon knew who her targets were. No mystery!
- What networks of influence exist in my organization? For Sharon, it was all about the people sitting at the top and the next level down.
- Who will make the final decision? Who on my map is closely aligned with this person? The CEO would not make it happen for Sharon without the majority on his team agreeing and actively supporting her. Before she began, Sharon had three of the five in support of her.

- Who will be most difficult to win over and why? Who may choose to block me? Sharon was clear on who the blockers were. In the end, she managed to win over one of the two.
- What political dynamics and extenuating circumstances must I keep in mind? Things change, and what works today will not work six months from now. (This is an important lens through which to view career and work dynamics.)
- How can I get started? Get real and start mapping out your situation. Write it down!

Sharon used her relationship map to efficiently network and become strategically aligned with the people who mattered most. Was she being calculating? Manipulative? No! She was being smart and effective. In fact, it was a large part of her job to get to know the executive team and work with them. One of the reasons Sharon got promoted so fast? She understood her executive colleagues, what they stood for, and how they were connected to each other and to her.

Relationship maps create a framework for understanding the network of professional contacts that surround us, and help us move ahead to forge the professional relationships that matter most.

3. Examine the culture

While a relationship map can serve as our strategy document, creating a bedrock of supporters also requires understanding the culture and norms within your organization. Ask yourself, is your culture hierarchical or informal? In many organizations, it is entirely acceptable to e-mail your boss's boss with a new business idea. In others, this type of off-the-cuff behavior is considered taboo and you need to go through your manager. Company conventions need not be followed to the letter every time, but it's essential to know the norms and be strategic in how you proceed. Understand who really makes the decisions.

Alice had been an executive at a Fortune 500 media corporation in New York City for nearly a decade when she set her sights on landing a very big job:

publisher of a national magazine. She had done her homework all along the way: she sought feedback about her performance and career potential, took several lateral positions to gain broad exposure and strategic experience, made her career aspirations known, built relationships with all the key players, took risks, built a coalition, and so on.

When her prized job became available, Alice wanted it and she stepped up to ask. She felt secure in the knowledge that she had done all that she needed to do. The day the decision was being made, she got the nod and was elated. She left the office having been secretly assured that the job was hers. However, when she returned to the office the next morning, fully expecting to read an announcement with her name in it, she found that the job had been given to someone else (another extremely deserving and smart woman!).

What happened? Over the course of twelve hours, the organizational structure had shifted and Alice's boss had changed roles. The new boss knew the other candidate much better, and he chose her for the role. Things change quickly when top jobs are at stake.

Moral of the story: you need widespread support, and you need to know everyone who has the power to either support or veto you.

Post mortem: if Alice had actually created a relationship map, and been completely honest with herself, she might have seen this coming and been slightly more prepared.

Take a close look at social customs and conventions and how they play out in your workplace. Things had always moved fast at Alice's corporation, and she might have anticipated this eleventh-hour power shift. Make notes at the bottom of your relationship map and build them into your professional plan.

4. Establish common ground

Strategic relationship building is made easier by listening up and learning something about the people around you—and using it to forge an authentic connection. As you work through your relationship map, do your homework and determine what information will help you connect in a win-win way.

Beth, a woman we've coached, is a self-proclaimed "Boston-born, Irish-Catholic from a large family, who grew up spending weekends at Fenway Park." Beth loves to talk about Boston. When she learned that her incoming boss was a Red Sox fan, she saw an easy opportunity to connect—and she seized it.

"The first thing we talked about was baseball, and it was an instant ice breaker," she said. "It created a real connection and we were able to build a relationship based on shared interests."

This strategy really works; however, we would argue that finding common ground may be different for women and men. As mentioned previously, research by Deborah Tannen shows that whereas women use similarities to connect, men connect through sports and competition. Although you don't need to join a fantasy football team to network effectively with male colleagues, it's important to accommodate gender differences in your networking strategy.

An apt way to make this work is to find out what is important to male and female influencers. Remember, Sharon won over one of her chief detractors by collaborating on a project they both wanted to advance. Be it baseball or travel, find something to talk about or sponsor a project together. Common ground helps form strong relationships and becomes the basis for future influence.

5. Take action!

The best advice is usually the simplest: *avoid overthinking things and just do something.* Next time you are killing time waiting for a plane, write down key relationships. Don't eat lunch alone at your desk. Don't stand on the sidelines during group discussions. Look at your relationship map and use your time wisely. One simple way to make this mind shift stick is to set a goal for yourself. Challenge yourself to meet with one new colleague each week. Boost your momentum in this situation by finding someone who is masterful at forming strategic alliances and watch that person work. Better yet, sit with him or her and ask for advice. Once you become accustomed to being friendly and exhibiting confidence, you'll learn that most people want to help. Are there times when you get shut out of a conversation? Has your meeting with the CEO been canceled *again*? Yes, everyone gets flattened sometimes—don't give up.

The good news is that building relationships gets easier with practice. If you engage with influencers every chance you get over a six-month period, imagine how much progress you'll make. Making strategic connections has a cumulative effect and so does influence. Soon, the payoff will become apparent and you'll be an influencer yourself.

Executive Summary

- Relationships form the foundation for influence.
- Working hard is never enough. Forging professional relationships and alignments is the real "hard work" we need to do.
- It is more important to get to know colleagues and determine if there is common ground from which to move forward than it is to like people and be liked.
- Taking difficult professional interactions personally makes it harder for us to establish the influence we need to lead.
- Creating a relationship map adds rigor to our process and helps us identify influencers.
- Common ground helps us forge strong relationships, and it becomes the basis for future influence.
- Take action. From achieving job growth to forging consensus for your agenda, relationships pay dividends.

6

Scenario Thinking

*For me, it is always important that I go
through all the possible options for a decision.*

—ANGELA MERKEL

WHAT WOULD YOU DO RIGHT now if you got a call from the Big Boss offering you a new job opportunity or a big role of some kind? His offer is about a role you've never considered. It is not directly on your current career path, and it is very high profile. What would your inner voice say to you? What stories would you tell yourself? Assuming that you would have the presence of mind to thank the Big Boss for his offer and tell him you need a day to think it over, what would your next steps be?

If you are like many of the women we coach, you are good at what you do and you like the people you work with. You have worked hard to gain professional recognition in your field and you are always thinking about your next move. Yet your current arrangement at work is comfortable and suits your lifestyle. A new role would entail navigating a steep learning curve, working harder, getting to know a new team, and potentially spending more time away from your family. Because the role is high profile, there is the risk of incurring disagreement and criticism. If you failed, it would be a very public failure. What will you decide? More importantly, *how* will you decide?

Let's look to an executive working at one of our client companies to see how she responded. Then, later in the chapter, we will explore how another woman we coach handled a similar opportunity.

> *Yvette was a senior vice president and regional sales leader at a U.S.-based publishing company. She was the company's most outstanding sales manager. She was not only respected by her staff and clients, she was loved. One of her clients told us, "I would do anything for Yvette Williams. She's in a class by herself."*
>
> *A few months after we met Yvette, there was a change in leadership at the top of her company. The CEO retired and was succeeded by an outstanding internal candidate. A month or so later, the new CEO promoted Yvette's boss, David, to a higher-level position. In short order, David did exactly what everyone expected him to do—he asked Yvette to accept the role of national sales leader. It was a major promotion into a highly visible role that everyone agreed she was qualified for. She would sit on the executive committee and assume national responsibilities. And, by the way, she would be only the second woman on the executive committee.*
>
> *Yvette's response to the job offer was trepidation. She hadn't seen this coming. She couldn't envision herself on the executive committee. When David sat down to talk with her, Yvette fixated on why she was not ready and listed all the things she didn't know. She said she didn't think she could do the new job and she didn't want to let him down. David reassured her, saying that he knew her well and was certain she would be successful in this new role. He needed her. He even offered to have her continue to report to him directly until she felt more comfortable, and suggested getting her some executive coaching. He reminded her that an opportunity like this comes around very infrequently. Yvette asked for some time to think it over.*
>
> *What was going on here? When we talked to Yvette, she explained, "I don't see myself in a high-level role yet; maybe someday....I'm just not ready and I*

have a lot going on." She went on to say, "I was taken by surprise and I wasn't prepared for the offer.... Honestly, it's not even an option." Yvette called David and turned down his offer.

There's nothing inherently wrong with turning down a promotion or an assignment. If the opportunity is not strategically aligned with your career goals and interests, say no more. But that wasn't the case here. Yvette allowed herself to get caught up in self-doubt. She did not stop to analyze the situation and think through all of her options. What a mess! Although Yvette is still at the same organization today, she regrets making this important decision in such a hasty manner.

Influence and confidence are inextricably linked. In this case, being strategic could have changed the outcome for Yvette because it would have enabled her to envision all of the possible alternatives of the situation.

THE UNWRITTEN RULE: Create Possibilities

In our work with women leaders, we talk about *scenario thinking*, the ability to see multiple alternatives at once and react fast in response to opportunities. One of the women we interviewed for our research describes scenario thinking this way:

> *I have to see five moves out.... If I do #1, then so-and-so is going to be for it and so-and-so is going to be against it. If I do #2, what's going to happen? If I do #3, what's going to happen? I try to be Sherlock Holmes and run each scenario out to decide how I'm going to move forward. I have to put the mental time into examining various alternatives in my head.*
>
> *Also, you must figure out people's motivations. You must do the deep listening and the deep thought and figure out what is it that they are driven by.*

Yvette wouldn't let herself accept a career opportunity that was so well suited to her experience and aspirations. Her story is a bit extreme, but we've seen this happen enough times to take note. Uncertainty, doubt, and fear can blind even the best of us and make it difficult for us to see that we are more agile than we think.

LIMITING BELIEFS That Decrease Our Options

How we think about ourselves has an outsized impact on what we can achieve. As we have seen, exposing negative thoughts and turning them around elevates our confidence and meaningfully increases our opportunities for advancement.

"I'm not ready."

"I'll be exposed as a fraud."

"I'm not ready"

Many of us become so blocked by uncertainty and fear that we can't picture a path to success. We worry about the complexity of our lives and are concerned about failing and letting everyone down. Sometimes we get so wedded to our current situation, as Yvette did, that we fixate on the default option. The same holds true for all types of professional challenges in addition to career decisions. It can be difficult to cut through our limiting beliefs and envision multiple scenarios for success when we are trying to lead a project, find a sponsor, or deliver a key account.

Another dynamic that makes us less open to considering "riskier" alternatives is our status as minorities in the executive suite. Because of our underrepresentation, we are aware that all eyes are on us. For women, and for all minorities, the cost of failure is higher than for our white male colleagues. We feel we need to do everything right because we're being judged more publicly and more harshly. We stay on the default path, where we know we can succeed, because we don't want to be "the woman who couldn't make it."

There's no single way to succeed, and locking ourselves into a black-or-white way of thinking drastically limits our options. It not only stifles creativity but also prevents us from seeing the entire spectrum of nuanced alternatives that exist between the obvious extremes. Black-or-white thinking is a sign that you are stuck and missing the nimbleness that comes with full-color thinking.

Yvette opted out of her big promotion because it didn't fit into the rigid plan she had for her career at that particular time. Sticking closely to one plan may seem like a safe and smart way to go, but it actually compounds the pressure.

One way to escape the either-or trap is to practice becoming comfortable with cognitive dissonance. Roger Martin, dean of the Rotman School of Management, argues that the best leaders today work at holding "two conflicting ideas in constructive tension."[1] This practice is diametrically opposed to all-or-nothing extremes. Holding two or more opposing ideas in your mind helps you find creative solutions to complex problems. According to Martin, "integrative thinkers" search for "creative resolutions of tensions, rather than accepting unpleasant trade-offs...and they keep the entire problem firmly in mind while working on its individual parts."[2]

What We Heard in Our Interviews

"You have to do some scenario thinking. Think through each path, figure out which one will work best, and then get ready for the unexpected. You have to think through different ways to proceed."

—ALICIA ROSE, GLOBAL LEAD CLIENT SERVICES PARTNER FOR AMERICAN EXPRESS, DELOITTE & TOUCHE

"You must roll through the options and spend the time to think through the ramifications of each one."

—MALE SENIOR EXECUTIVE

"I'll be exposed as a fraud"

We mentioned the impostor syndrome in chapter 2. The biggest symptom of the impostor syndrome is the ongoing fear of being exposed as a "fraud." In fact, when we described the impostor syndrome to Yvette, she said, "That's me. That's exactly how I feel."

Most of us are not impacted in a permanent way by this syndrome. Yet many women we work with are held back by an out-of-sync self-image.

When the voice in our head is not in sync with our abilities and professional success, a few things can happen. First, we feel like we're not ready—not ready to throw our hat in the ring for a promotion, not ready to dissent in a business meeting, and so on. We're paralyzed and silenced. A second reaction is fear. Fear results in what we call *default thinking*. Our lack of confidence keeps us from being creative and looking at all our options. Following the default path causes us to "lock down" and therefore miss creative alternatives, options, and opportunities. Our fear and nagging feeling of inferiority cause us to always play it safe. Yvette played it safe because she did not want to "let everyone down." The irony of her decision is that that's exactly what she did.

We coach women to set the voices in their heads straight. Create a narrative inside your mind that is empowering. Look at yourself objectively, own your assets and accomplishments, and don't hide behind the relative safety of the default path.

Questions for Reflection

➡ Is your inner voice your friend or your foe? How do you know? What is it telling you?

➡ When have you taken a calculated risk that worked out well? What did you do to get comfortable with your decision?

➡ Who can you go to for input and advice when hard decisions arise? Are these people able to be objective about the situation? Are they able to be totally candid with you?

STRATEGIES for Creating Possibilities

One of the best "scenario thinkers" we know, Claudette, learned this skill through trial and error.

> *Several years back, when Claudette was a young partner at a Chicago-based firm, the demands of being on the fast track hit her hard. The better Claudette performed, the more work the senior partners passed down to her. Just about the time she was starting to doubt her capacity to manage the pressure, she was asked by the CEO to lead the high-visibility Corporate Women's Program (CWP).*
>
> *The CWP was designed to bring together women from across the organization to mentor female associates, share best practices, and create a national community of support. Managed by a different female leader each term, the two-year role was perceived as a high-visibility appointment and a vote of confidence. For Claudette, it was an opportunity to demonstrate her leadership talent. The problem? The CWP workload was in addition to the client work she already had on her plate.*
>
> *After taking the weekend to think it over, Claudette accepted the new responsibility. She felt passionate about the work of the CWP and believed she could grow the program to have a greater impact at the firm. "The alternative was to pass on the opportunity, and it did not seem like the right option for me or the firm," she told us.*
>
> *At first, Claudette took the default path. In prior years, the CWP director managed the program just as she would a client account. She did most of the planning and execution herself. The work culminated in three regional meetings per year, plus one massive conference at year-end and numerous other networking activities. Claudette would be the emcee and grand master at each of the four meetings.*
>
> *It took her six weeks to realize that this approach was a no-go. Past CWP leads had much less client work than Claudette. She was exhausted, her accounts were suffering, and all the groundwork left her with no time to show her face as the program's leader. Claudette came to her coach in tears, saying, "I never should have agreed to take this role. I'm afraid I'm going to fail."*

We worked with Claudette to calm the negative voices in her head and tap into her confidence by recalling her past accomplishments. We also reminded Claudette of her rationale for accepting the new role: she had big plans for the CWP.

Now she was in a better frame of mind—more empowered, more confident. Claudette took a deep breath and stepped up. She began by getting clear about her desired outcome. Then she mapped out a few different ways to approach the CWP position. She came up with three scenarios.

Claudette's CWP Scenarios

Desired outcome: Drive success and growth for the CWP, enhance my reputation as a leader in the firm, and continue to be an outstanding client service partner.

SCENARIO 1: **Likely Case**
Incremental change for the CWP: Keep the program design the same but change the rollout by recruiting additional leaders to get involved in the CWP and assist in the implementation of events.

SCENARIO 2: **Best Case**
Radical change for the CWP: Change both the implementation and program design based on an improved vision and an expansion of the program.

SCENARIO 3: **Worst Case**
I am unable to create momentum for the program and I am replaced as head of the CWP program.

Claudette considered the three scenarios. She imagined how each one would play out and how she would measure success. For the likely case, she decided that a key success metric would be increased volunteer involvement. She even made a list of the specific leaders she would be targeting. For the best case, Claudette got creative. Her metrics centered on securing broad involvement from both male and female leaders, plus some additional outreach activities with clients. She did not know the exact details of the scenario, but she let herself dream big.

For the worst case, Claudette considered what she would do if everything went awry and she was removed from her CWP role. As she considered that scenario, she realized two things. First, this scenario was *highly unlikely*. It was based primarily on her own fear of failure as opposed to any real facts or probabilities. Second, Claudette realized that if the worst case did happen, she would still be okay. She wouldn't be fired from the firm, and she would still have her clients. Yes, it would be embarrassing and she would need to repair her reputation internally, but overall, *she would be fine*.

Once Claudette had thought through her scenarios, she decided to create momentum around scenario 1, the likely case. First, she invited key female leaders to play a role in publicizing and planning the CWP. Second, she recruited six female partners to manage the regional events on a volunteer basis. Third, she recruited a group of associates to plan the annual conference. In the end, they expanded the conference. The women partners spent a day and a half together focusing on key topics related to supporting each other across the firm.

Claudette's first year as CWP leader was a success, and the enthusiasm across the firm was noted by the CEO. Claudette was proud of what she and her colleagues had accomplished. Despite her success, however, Claudette saw room for improvement. In the subsequent year, she moved on to scenario 2, the best case.

With her colleagues feeling confident and empowered in each of the regions, Claudette stepped up her leadership role. She doubled the size of the annual conference to include *all* female partners and directors. She initiated CWP awards to recognize outstanding performance for women across the firm. Finally, she took the unprecedented step of inviting twenty male leaders to attend the annual conference. She called the men "CWP Champions." They were honored to be included and learned a lot from attending the meeting. A final update was to institute a series of CWP events to benefit the firm's female clients. All of these actions dramatically increased the impact of the program. Because Claudette was able to attract new stakeholders, many more people felt they "owned" a part of the success of the CWP.

Scenario thinking set Claudette up to be creative, bold, and prepared for multiple paths. She was able to manage her fear and modify her course in real time. Claudette gained stature and influence as a leader, and she was widely considered "a huge success" in the role of CWP leader.

STEPS for Scenario Thinking

We coach women to become comfortable with scenario thinking by experimenting with "what if" possibilities. In most cases, we want women to use scenario thinking as a *lens* as opposed to a major planning exercise. The idea is to discipline yourself to examine the surrounding landscape for multiple possible options, and then plan your actions accordingly. Scenario thinking is not about foreseeing the future; it is about adjusting your plans and decisions in response to real-time events and complexity.

STEPS for Scenario Thinking

1. Banish fear.
2. Determine your outcome.
3. Create your options.
4. Identify and assess your stakeholders.
5. Respond to your constraints.
6. Remain nimble and proceed.

1. Banish fear

This is the most important step because fear is a distortion that can stop us cold. When we let it take over, we become reactive and emotional instead of creative and practical. Yvette went directly into "default mode" and turned down a once-in-a-lifetime promotion because of her debilitating fear of failure. Claudette had fears, too, but she worked through them. She regained her confidence, used her optimism, and replaced the negative voice in her head with a positive message.

2. Determine your outcome

When the stakes are high you need to spend some time on preparation. Think creatively about the outcome you are looking for, focusing strictly on your ideal end-result, as opposed to how you will achieve it. Be specific and keep it simple. Claudette's desired outcome was: Drive success and growth for the CWP, enhance my reputation as a leader, and continue to be an outstanding partner in the firm.

3. Create your options

Consider three ways to achieve your outcomes. We suggest mapping out a best case, worst case, and likely case. In your likely case, things proceed as expected with nary a speed bump or unexpected event. Simply thinking through that scenario will help clarify your expectations and queue up your plan. The worst case involves imagining every major snafu you can think of (all hell breaks loose, you're left holding the bag, and so on). Considering this extreme helps you prepare for the worst, even as you expect the best—you are ready for any eventuality. Finally, your best case can be anything you want—so long as it satisfies your objective and is outside the box. Brainstorm the most innovative ways to proceed and see what sticks. If you had asked Claudette early on if she expected to invite men to the women's conference, she would have said no way...but it worked!

As you map out your options, remember that scenario thinking needs to be dynamic. As demonstrated in Figure 10, try to anticipate what may happen over time, taking other people and outside forces into account.

FIGURE 10   Scenario Thinkers Are
Nimble, Proactive, and Prepared

Keep in mind that it is possible that none of your scenarios will come to pass exactly as you've mapped them out. The idea is to consider the possibilities and identify ways to move ahead.

4. Identify and assess your stakeholders

Consider your outcomes with key stakeholders in mind: How will peers, competitors, and clients impact the likelihood of achieving your goal? In what ways might their views impact your decisions and help or harm your chances of success? Claudette needed to please her bosses, engage women in the firm, and manage her clients. Taking this even further, think about what is most important to your stakeholders and where you interests overlap with theirs. A male executive we interviewed described how this works for him: "I had to figure out early on: What is this person's motivation? I had to listen deeply and probe to become skillful at understanding what they wanted and what motivated them."

5. Respond to your constraints

Think about project deadlines, end dates such as fiscal-year goals, and any personal timing constraints you may face. Do any of these dates have the potential to shift? Claudette had an annual conference, a two-year term, and other fluid client-oriented deadlines to factor into her planning.

What else is occurring inside your business, or outside in the competitive landscape, that might impact success? Constraints (and opportunities) might include budgeting and resources, competing products or programs, or even legislation that will affect the success of your plan.

After you consider your stakeholders and constraints, think about the specific if-then rules or options you would build into your scenarios. *If* my budget is slashed, *then* I will look for outside funding; *if* my customers push back, *then* I will decrease the price; and so on.

6. Remain nimble and proceed

A primary point of scenario planning is to clear a safe path for action. Having peered into the future to consider what might occur, you are now fully prepared to proceed and can advance when the light is green.

As you confidently move forward, remember that the process should remain iterative: constantly scan the environment, remain dynamic, and be ready to adjust and adapt. When something starts working, stand poised to leverage the momentum. When Claudette recruited volunteers to join her in leading each of the CWP's regional events, it was viewed as a considerable early win. She was later able to build on that and include both female and male sponsors to grow the program in directions that no one would have predicted was possible.

During her tenure as the CWP lead, Claudette went from being seen as a future star to becoming an influential leader who earned the trust and respect of executives all across the company. She was able to proceed with confidence, take risks, and respond to opportunities.

Most professions and industries are in some type of transition or flux. Things change fast. The most successful female leaders we know are flexible and open minded, and they realize that there's never only one response to an opportunity. Being decisive amid uncertainty, leaning into unexpected opportunities, and seeing multiple paths to success are all a part of achieving influence and working toward achieving the Influence Effect.

Executive Summary

- Default thinking limits our options, stifles creativity, and prevents us from seeing the entire spectrum of nuanced alternatives that exist between the obvious extremes.
- Creating an empowering narrative inside our mind makes it simpler to seize opportunities and bypass barriers.
- Scenario thinking is not about foreseeing the future; it is about adjusting our plans and decisions in response to real-time events and complexity. It is a dynamic process.
- Scenario thinking is iterative and dynamic as we run through our if-then options.
- Staying nimble to seize opportunities requires confidence, conviction, and a willingness to take action.

Influence Loops

You are constantly in the mode of influencing in order to get things done. You must build support, seek advice and counsel. You must seek buy-in.

—KAREN DAHUT, EXECUTIVE VICE
PRESIDENT, BOOZ ALLEN HAMILTON

When Sara arrived at work, she found she had a "new opportunity." She currently managed HR for the wealth management division of a large U.S. investment bank. That morning, her boss gave her additional responsibility for all human resources functions for an investment banking company that her bank had recently acquired.

Sara had managed mergers before this, but in the past there was more ramp-up time for planning, and the businesses in question had been smaller and less complex. She would need to reorganize the operational aspects of the combined businesses, reassign staff, get up to speed on entirely new processes, and create a new organization chart.

Three things were immediately clear to Sara:

1. The HR teams of both banks were nervous about the integration. Many individuals felt the teams would need to remain entirely separate to ensure that important projects and "sacred" processes were maintained.
2. The CEO of the newly combined organization wanted the HR integration managed without additional expense or negative publicity. He was especially concerned about morale taking a hit.
3. Stakeholders in the business units were looking to Sara to pull the two HR groups together quickly so HR could help lead the business units through their own reorganization process.

This was the career turning point Sara had been waiting for, and she said she felt "nervous but up to the task." The first thing she did was find a large whiteboard to sketch out a plan for organizing the new division. She used black marker for the parts she felt were nonnegotiable, blue for the pieces that were slightly more speculative, and green for the parts that were entirely open to input.

Over the next several weeks, she visited each of the HR teams (old and new) separately, flying in remote workers and field agents to get people into the room and allow them to talk face to face. E-mail would be faster, but she knew it would not be effective in changing minds and getting people on board. She brought the original whiteboard drawing into each meeting to signify that her plans were still fluid and she needed their feedback and expertise.

She met with each HR group, listened to their ideas and concerns, and factored in the changes she thought would work. She then revisited the CEO and his executive team and made adjustments based on their input. She went on to meet with the finance and operations leaders and factored in the logistics that were of concern to them. All of these meetings required considerable time and a great deal of listening. Sara and her team worked tirelessly to accommodate all reasonable changes in the plan. Sara then returned to each of the groups to share the updated version of the plan. Each meeting generated more input, and Sara's collaborative approach built trust among all parties.

Finally, Sara was ready for a full-day meeting with the combined HR organization. She walked through the new organizational chart, the timeline, and *other specifics. In addition to outlining what would change in the new organ-ization, she focused on the past accomplishments of both HR groups and made a point to talk about the things that would not need to change.*

After that meeting, it was a done deal. Not everyone was entirely comfortable with the new organization, but they bought in. They saw that the process had been open and that they had input. The way Sara handled the integration sent a signal to employees that the corporate culture of the new organ-ization was open and collaborative and took the needs and ideas of each person seriously.

THE UNWRITTEN RULE: Use Influence Loops to Create a Coalition for Change

Sara's story illustrates a powerful tool called *influence loops*. Stated simply, influ-ence loops are a systematic process to get input from multiple groups of stake-holders. Influence loops are the beginning of coalition building. The intent is to coalesce groups around ideas by sharing openly, soliciting feedback, and creat-ing a process for input. Sara used influence loops when she aced the HR integra-tion at the bank.

As Figure 11 illustrates, Sara went out multiple times to numerous groups with an evolving message. She used influence loops to test her ideas and bring people on board. She started with the loops of both the new and acquired HR leaders, which consisted of individuals on two separate teams. Sara used the loops to bring them up to speed, get their input, and help diffuse their anxiety. Her third loop included her champions: her boss and the CEO. She presented her plans at a high level and received the go-ahead to proceed. Sara's fourth loop was her key stakeholder loop. She met with IT, operations, and financial leaders to get their thinking on logistics and execution. She revisited each loop multi-ple times as her plans became more concrete, and each new pass achieved a different objective—neutralizing resistance, getting feedback, securing buy-in, achieving closure, and so on.

Sara used what she learned from each consecutive influence loop to im-prove her plan and her messaging. She was listening, learning, and responding

FIGURE 11   Influence Loops

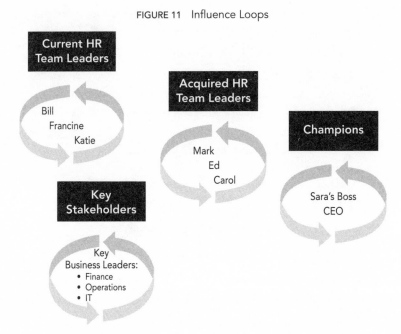

the entire time. She went back and forth between her HR team (loop 1), the acquired HR team (loop 2), her champions (loop 3), and other key stakeholders (loop 4) numerous times. Ultimately, she had a sound plan that had broad support.

Influence loops are simple and effective and, as Sara demonstrated, they enable you to improve your plans as you bring people on board. In order to create a coalition, your stakeholders need to be heard and they need to be included throughout the process. Ultimately, they become as excited as you are.

LIMITING BELIEFS That Curb Our Influence

Being asked to lead a complex and potentially unpopular change initiative like Sara's will probably activate a host of limiting beliefs in our heads: "I'm not ready." "They'll know I'm an impostor." "This takes too much time." "I shouldn't ask for help." These negative messages are discussed elsewhere in this book. There are two additional limiting beliefs that we want to address head-on right now.

"I don't like bargaining/selling/asking."

"I have the CEO's support, and that's all I need."

"I don't like bargaining/selling/asking"

Why do certain people get chosen for leadership positions? Yes, some people are chosen for the wrong reasons. However, many leaders are chosen because they know how to *drive change* successfully in the organization. Think about it. The primary reason organizations need leaders is so that the organization and its people can remain nimble and responsive in the face of massive and often unpredictable changes in the marketplace.

Being good at driving change means being good at selling ideas and influencing other people's behavior.

It's no major surprise that women have exceptional selling talents. In fact, Tom Peters said that women make better salespeople than men.[1] What we've found in coaching senior-level women, however, is a dichotomy. Women working in sales jobs are the best in class at what they do—and they love it. Yet, women in nonsales roles tell us they would prefer a trip to the dentist over selling. Unfortunately, selling is one of those things—like public speaking—that we avoid at our own peril. It is a requirement for leading change in any organization.

Changing minds requires a willingness to sell your ideas. It also requires making deals. The women we interviewed for our research professed a disdain for side deals and bargaining tactics. They felt that making deals was sneaky and dishonest, especially when they happened behind the scenes. This type of thinking calls for a simple mind shift. Several successful women we interviewed equated bargaining with being deliberate and disciplined, not dishonest.

We know that selling, doing deals, and contracting with colleagues is how business works. Thinking about these as *tools* as opposed to *tricks* makes them more palatable to us as women.

"I have the CEO's support, and that's all I need"

You are excited. You have a mandate and funding from the CEO to lead an important change initiative. This is your chance to enhance your reputation and manage a high-profile project within your company. You have a well-researched master plan for new processes, and technology that will vastly improve efficiency. You have an ambitious timeline and team members to help you. You are anxious to get started. This is going to be great!

Wait a minute. Not so fast. You've got the CEO's backing, but that's not all you'll need to be successful. You also need to bring other key stakeholders on board. Any major change initiative is also a shift in organizational culture, and cultural change takes time and patience.

Organizational culture is made up of the norms, mores, traditions, and unwritten rules in an organization. A skilled influencer knows her organization's culture and navigates through it. If not, culture can stop a change agent in her tracks. The legendary Peter Drucker allegedly said that "culture eats strategy for breakfast," and many management experts agree with the idea that strategy and culture need to be aligned for any change process to succeed.[2]

> ### Questions for Reflection
>
> ⇒ What is your strategy to lead change?
>
> ⇒ How will you persuade others to accept and champion the change?
>
> ⇒ How have you taken the current corporate culture into account?
>
> ⇒ Do you know who the change "resisters" will be? What is your plan to win them over?

STRATEGIES for Creating Influence Loops

Using influence loops is an effective way for women to drive change, change minds, and gain ongoing support. This smart tool leverages women's considerable strengths and works particularly well in environments with competing agendas and multiple levels of power and control.

STRATEGIES for Creating Influence Loops

1. Build trust before you need it.
2. Identify key stakeholders.
3. Prepare yourself.
4. Have face-to-face meetings.
5. Repeat!
6. Use the gift of the gap.

1. Build trust before you need it

The reason we teach women to use influence loops is that it builds trust before you need it. Influence loops can be used to surround yourself with trusted allies in advance of creating any agenda that you need to elevate. In fact, they can be used to build a strong layer of support for your career—not unlike the scaffolding we described in chapter 3. Because of that, trust is a key component of any effective influence loop strategy.

Yet trust can be elusive. Peter Block, author of *The Empowered Manager: Positive Political Skills at Work*, asserts that there are two dimensions that impact our ability to influence others: trust and agreement.[3] According to Block, influence is much easier if the trust is high, *even* when there is significant disagreement. It is important to understand that trust and agreement are not the same thing. Disagreement without trust is usually a showstopper. Of course, trust is easier to develop *before* there is disagreement. As we said in chapter 4, the power of the informal can go a long way toward developing trust. Be intentional in developing trusted relationships—whether you are using the informal settings discussed in chapter 4, the relationship maps described in chapter 5, or the influence loops suggested here. All of these tools help to create trust, even when agreement is withheld. In fact, disagreement can actually be helpful because it forces the parties to look deeper to find the path to a greater outcome.

2. Identify key stakeholders

We've already described how Sara identified key stakeholders for her HR merger project. There were four groups in her influence loops:

1. The CEO and Sara's boss, who were sponsors of the project
2. The newly acquired HR leaders
3. The HR leaders who were already at the bank
4. Other functional stakeholders (finance, IT, and operations)

Identifying your stakeholders is really very simple. Ask yourself, who are the individuals and groups of people who will be affected by this change? Your list will dictate your different influence loops. As you make out your list, be sure to ask your colleagues, "Who else do I need to touch base with?"

3. Prepare yourself

We've put together the key questions to ask yourself as you cycle through the process of using influence loops.

BEFORE YOU BEGIN, ASK YOURSELF THE FOLLOWING:

- Am I open to changing my ideas based on stakeholders' input?
- Am I willing to revisit my ideas multiple times with numerous key people until the best solution is found?
- Am I acting with integrity and ready to build trust with others?
- Am I vulnerable and courageous enough to seek help?

AS YOU PLAN YOUR LOOPS, ASK YOURSELF THE FOLLOWING:

- What is the intention of my strategy, change, or idea? What will be different as a result?
- Who are my key stakeholders?
- What parts of my plan are fixed and what is negotiable?
- What is the appetite for change in this organization?
- Who are the potential resisters around me?

FINALLY, BEFORE YOU ROLL OUT THE FINAL PLAN, ASK YOURSELF THE FOLLOWING:

- Have I communicated repeatedly with my stakeholders? (You don't want them to be surprised.)
- Have I gathered input from people who may resist or have concerns about my plan?
- Have I listened to the gossip about me or my plan?
- Have I considered everyone who needs to be on board for change to succeed?
- Have I identified some early wins?

4. Have face-to-face meetings

An important aspect of leading change is building trust and consensus with key stakeholders. This means that your influence loops should be in-person meetings, whenever possible. Why? Because an in-person meeting signals that something important is going on and that the people at the meeting are also important. In the business world today, most meetings are virtual. It is not easy to build trust and agreement with people over the phone or e-mail. You need to be able to read body language and energy to determine how someone is reacting to the discussion. Your job as the change leader is to connect with and listen to your stakeholders. As you continue to conduct influence loops, your stakeholders will begin to see themselves in your vision. That's when you'll know you have succeeded.

5. Repeat!

This bears repeating: influence loops are not "one and done." Yes, they require an investment of time and energy. However, they save us headaches now and reduce the number of blockers in our path later.

We, as women, are innate relationship builders. As such, influence loops suit our needs as a practical strategy we can adopt and customize. In addition, they make it easier for us to be transactional, problem solve, and move forward when our agenda hits a snag or encounters resistance. In fact, with influence loops, resistance is addressed in advance and blockers are brought on board with the change. This is an especially effective tool when we get stuck, with little idea about what our next move might be. Make a loop and listen! Then revisit the loop and listen some more.

6. Use the gift of the gap

Influence loops won't eliminate all pain points on the way to achieving buy-in. There are times when we need to regroup. We call this the *gift of the gap*. The space in between loops offers a chance for reflection. Gaps create opportunities to think deeply as opposed to bulldozing ahead. *We can then refine and perhaps redesign our response, or even create a new approach altogether.*

The gift of the gap is important when you need to let something marinate. Whether it is a new opportunity, a career change, or constructive feedback, time to reflect leads to better decisions.

A gap is particularly important in emotional situations or in dealing with difficult personalities.

Tonya is a bank executive. The culture at the office where she works (as senior vice president of consumer banking) is conservative. They have a clear hierarchy, formal attire, and a mostly male team of top executives. In fact, Tonya was the only woman on the finance leadership team.

Tonya was working on a new mortgage platform that would involve the entire finance team. She took her time building a coalition of support using four key stakeholders. As expected, she encountered resistance. One person in particular, Bob, the bank's operations leader, was known to be a bully, and Tonya knew he would be a problem.

Sure enough, Bob appeared unannounced at one of Tonya's meetings— which was essentially an influence loop. He sat quietly at first, but then he began to make snide remarks about the project and how she was managing it. It was clear that his remarks were designed to embarrass her in front of her stakeholders. As Bob went on, Tonya reached a boiling point and was close to losing her composure. With extreme effort, Tonya put on the brakes and maintained control of herself. She quietly but firmly said they would discuss his concerns one on one. If she ever needed the gift of the gap, it was now.

Tonya waited. A few days later, she saw Bob walking by her office. She stood up and asked him to stop in. (It was important for Tonya to be in her own office—on her "turf.") She approached the conversation with confidence and poise, and she stated simply, "The next time you want to attend one of my meetings, I insist that you let me know in advance. I would like to discuss your concerns in a respectful way. You are more likely to get what you want if you act professionally." Bob was caught off guard and said very little. After that, Tonya reviewed what she felt were his objective concerns about the project, and they managed to have a civil conversation.

Tonya and Bob never became allies, but he never tried the power game again, either. Ultimately, Tonya received the support she needed for her mortgage platform. The gift of the gap was a game changer.

Building coalitions and changing minds seldom happens overnight. That's why influence loops work—they have a cumulative effect. The gap in between loops can strengthen your case as you accumulate more information and greater support.

We know that the process of learning influence loops is not easy. In fact, it is complex, almost like three-dimensional chess. It requires you to look at situations from multiple perspectives and plan many moves ahead. It requires you to be both creative and savvy. It demands discipline, maturity, and persistence. Using influence loops is not a requirement for every small change project, but it is a necessity for the big ones.

What Our Interviews Revealed

"To work to strategize your outcome, it's a phone call, not an email—it's 'a conversation.' You ask questions, and then you ask, 'Who else should I talk to?'"

—SARAH GEORGE, SENIOR VICE PRESIDENT AND HUMAN RESOURCES LEADER, WELLS FARGO

"Men are much better at forming alliances by playing into what others' goals are."

—KATY HOLLISTER, MANAGING PARTNER, STRATEGY, GLOBAL TAX AND LEGAL, DELOITTE

"My politics is about getting my initiatives advanced, to get my colleagues to invest time, money, or energy to help get one of my initiatives accomplished."

—DEBRA PLOUSHA MOORE, SYSTEM CHIEF OF STAFF, CAROLINAS HEALTHCARE SYSTEM

"Men know they have to put together a marketing campaign around their idea or initiative. Women believe others will align because it is the right thing to do."

—FEMALE EXECUTIVE

Executive Summary

- Influence loops are a systematic way to reach out to multiple levels of contacts and stakeholders. It is a campaign to share your idea, gain feedback, and accumulate buy-in.
- Doing deals and contracting with colleagues to drive change is how business works. We need to look at these tactics for change as tools as opposed to tricks.
- The toughest part of any change project is understanding the corporate culture. The best change agents show their appreciation for past accomplishments and customs, even while they move to create a culture shift.
- Leading change across a team or business is not an individual endeavor. It requires creating coalitions and unifying them to the cause.
- Using influence loops can help you build trust before you need it.

8

Momentum

Momentum is really a leader's best friend.
Sometimes it's the only difference between
winning and losing.

—JOHN MAXWELL

ONE OF OUR COACHING CLIENTS, Denise, is an executive at a large medical instruments firm. When we first met Denise, she told us about a complex project she conceived some months back.

As someone who's known by colleagues to be serious, organized, and above all innovative, no one was surprised when Denise stepped forward with a visionary idea. Her idea was to build a new platform with a "dashboard" to connect and measure in real time the sales of their various medical devices and therapies. The system would deliver data to sales reps and marketers and allow them to see which products were gaining momentum at any given time. In the past, they had no way to quickly compare sales side by side and extract the deal specifics and pricing. This system had the potential to modernize their market-facing units.

The project was massive and would require new hardware and software, updated processes and training, and all-new performance metrics across the company. But the return on investment was compelling. If the system worked as planned, it would save money and increase customer satisfaction.

Denise presented the plan to her boss, who helped her sell it to the executive committee. After some trepidation, they gave Denise the green light and advanced enough capital to launch phase one of the project. Denise and her team worked eleven-hour days for weeks, doing the research and starting the design process. Everything looked promising. Then, something happened out of the blue that stunned Denise.

Denise's boss called her into his office and took her to task. "We're sixty days into your project.... Where are the results you promised us? I sold the executive team on this project and you haven't done your part to show progress. I'm putting the project on hold before it goes farther south."

After licking her wounds, Denise took a little time and, with some help from her coach, she figured out what had happened. She had developed her idea, analyzed the return on investment, and enrolled her stakeholders, but she had never checked back to communicate her interim progress with her boss or the executive committee. What's more, she never went far enough to sell her vision to the rest of the organization. She had no coalition behind her. The executive team saw a flurry of activity and expended resources, but there was no momentum that they could see. Denise had an aha moment. She realized that she needed to keep selling even *after* she had started the project. As much as Denise hated to admit it, her big project was delayed because she'd skipped crucial steps that would have helped her pick up steam and maintain support.

THE UNWRITTEN RULE: Manage
the Physics of Momentum

Momentum is the force or speed of an object in motion. In business, momentum is the increase in the rate of the development of a process.[1] Momentum keeps us moving forward and focused on our goals, instead of engaging in a frustrating series of starts and stops. As we've mentioned, it is harder for women to earn the badge of trust as leaders because, as research from Catalyst asserts, "gender stereotypes portray women as lacking the qualities that people commonly associate with effective leadership. This often creates false perceptions that women leaders just don't measure up to men in important ways."[2] For these systemic reasons, momentum is exceedingly important for women.

Instead of working harder for recognition, we coach women to build momentum by creating a state of energy and strategic forward movement. When it comes to momentum, a law of physics is in play. Energy builds with each milestone, and small wins eventually add up to influence.

LIMITING BELIEFS That Halt Our Momentum

Before moving on to master the strategies that actively help us create momentum, it's important to first acknowledge the limiting beliefs that hold us back.

"I get tired of the politics."

"I don't like to brag."

"It's like I'm driving through fog—I can't see clearly."

"I get tired of the politics"

In Greek mythology, Sisyphus is the iconic figure punished in Hades by being forced to roll an immense boulder uphill, only to see it roll back down, over and over again, for all of eternity.

Sound familiar? One of the women we interviewed likened the task of achieving momentum in her career to enduring this fruitless plight. "Even when I do my work extremely well, I feel like I'm being blocked. My momentum is constantly halted by difficult political dynamics that slow me down and minimize my accomplishments."

In many organizations, office politics is nonstop. It is that ongoing, continuous drumbeat of political dynamics that can wear some of us down and halt our momentum if we are not properly conditioned.

What the Women We Interviewed Said about the Things That Halt Their Professional Momentum

- "There are backroom deals happening that I'm not privy to. They cause me to be spinning my wheels."

- "We're having a tough year, resources are tight and you must lobby for them, and it takes constant effort."

- "I can't seem to get my voice heard in meetings no matter how loud I speak."

- "There is so much work to do, it is difficult to step back and take the precious time to plan how to change things."

"I don't like to brag"

No one likes a showboat, right? Well, that way of thinking only takes us so far. The reality is that our extreme modesty is another major momentum derailer. In fact, when we review 360-degree feedback reports, we are reminded that managers are not mind readers. They do not know all that their employees accomplish unless someone tells them. One boss said, "If you have done something great, let me know—I need to know the facts."

A 2014 study from the United Kingdom published in *Psychology of Women Quarterly* found that women are willing to celebrate the accomplishments of friends and colleagues but they are much less eager to engage in self-promotion.[3] This corroborates what we've found in our research, as well as what we witness every day in our coaching work. Many women put self-promotion in the "bad behavior" category, whereas our male colleagues find it simple to take credit for their own accomplishments. The female leadership paradigm is more about collaboration and teamwork, and less about showcasing individual success. This is something to be proud of, yet we need to be willing to own our achievements and build on them to fuel our momentum.

How do we do this? Write them down. Track them in an accomplishments log. What have you been working on lately? What challenges have you addressed? A consistent review, even monthly, can be invaluable. We are busy. We cannot remember our recent results and accomplishments, so reflect and track them. Then you have something to talk about.

We then tell women to find a way to talk about their accomplishments in a way that feels authentic to them. Some of us are great storytellers. Other people are adept at communicating in a slightly self-deprecating way so people barely know they are talking up their achievements. And then there are those of us who can just flat-out own our accomplishments without looking bad. Everyone has her own style. What's yours?

"It's like I'm driving through fog—I can't see clearly"

A third trend is a sense of being lost, or losing sight of our *vision*. It's very easy to get caught up in the everyday blizzard of agenda items punctuated by the occasional crisis. We lose our way and sense of direction. Then we are flying blind and proceeding wherever the wind takes us. But achieving momentum requires us to remain focused by managing our *direction, perspective*, and *alignment*.

The task of managing our *direction* relates to our advice regarding vision and checking the weather (chapter 2). Momentum needs to begin with the end in mind. Acknowledging that our ultimate target will sometimes shift, we need to periodically stop to aim ourselves in the right direction. Managing our *perspective* is about where we are in the journey and how far we have left to go. For example, our decisions—how we deal with setbacks and so on—should be different depending on whether we are at the beginning of the journey, near the very end, or somewhere in the middle. Finally, managing our *alignment* reminds us to make sure we achieve small wins early so we gain momentum faster and sustain it. Using navigational reminders such as these helps us reflect on the journey and not get lost in the complexity of so many overlapping tasks and commitments.

Questions for Reflection

➦ How are you moving forward in your career or with your business initiative? Have you stalled out, and if so, why?

➦ What are some recent successes or accomplishments? Consider tracking them in an accomplishments log.

➦ What political dynamics have you noticed? How are they affecting your ability to create small wins?

STRATEGIES to Manage the Physics of Momentum

Sapna was a training director at one of our client companies when she was asked to become chief learning officer. The CEO (Sapna's new boss) made it clear to her that the priority was to consolidate fifteen different training departments into one large division. It was necessary, he said, to create efficiencies and direct learning and development (L&D) funds toward new technologies.

Sapna took stock of the situation and set about building an overall learning infrastructure. What she found was that the unit managers were extremely upset about losing their training staff and unwilling to let go of their L&D funding without a fight. To make matters worse, Sapna had been their peer until very recently, when she was promoted above them. She could easily have pulled rank, but she understood that it might do more harm than good to use force over finesse.

"On the one hand, this was the CEO's priority and I didn't need to negotiate with each department head. I had the mandate," she told us. "On the other hand, how could I succeed in my new role without gaining the support of these managers?" Sapna asked.

Her first move was to propose a bold vision for learning and development that she hoped would begin to engage the naysayers. As part of her plan, she enlisted a financial analyst to make the business case for investing dollars in the new structure. The vision and numbers were compelling, but not enough to win over the skeptics. It was almost as if they were saying, "Show me."

Part two of the plan was to get her blockers involved in the implementation phase. Initially, she assigned a member of her team to be the ambassador and assist each business unit. Next, she created a board of advisers consisting of all of the department heads who had just given up their resources. This gave them a voice in the process and a seat at the table. Sapna went out of her way to ask for their input and ideas.

Together with the board of advisers, Sapna's team designed and created an innovative pilot program that not only involved key customers but also had clear benchmarks to indicate success. The soft launch of the pilot was a success and the numbers were solid. The next early win came when customer reviews were overwhelmingly positive. The advisers reported the results back to colleagues in their respective units. By that time, the advisers seemed to believe the entire new system was their own idea. In short, they were fully enrolled.

Sapna's early goal was to consolidate the fifteen training functions into a centralized operation. This led to efficiencies and cost savings. Next, an investment could be made in new technology solutions. Sapna then utilized this technology to measure results and create additional savings. The early wins accumulated and a transformational outcome resulted. In the end, momentum led to a big win.

The main difference between Sapna's story and Denise's was that Sapna carefully orchestrated her plan to include a string of critical early wins. She created energy by bringing these wins to her corporate stakeholders. This created a positive perception that the project was on its way to success. She also celebrated each of the wins with the wider team, and this built even more excitement. This cumulative effect developed momentum for Sapna, not only with the project but also in her career.

Sapna showed that managing the physics of your career is about creating and maintaining momentum by harnessing positive energy and results. It is also about *managing perception* to keep your career and its many pieces and parts moving ahead. You'll notice that the strategies we present next involve motion: moving forward, rising in the organization, and forging an agenda that can lift you up. Creating momentum is an active endeavor. Momentum is energy moving forward. It puts you in the driver's seat and makes you responsible for achieving success. It is this self-empowerment that enables you to rise above the limiting factors we talked about and begin to achieve influence at work.

STRATEGIES to Manage the Physics of Momentum

1. Center yourself.
2. Generate a string of small wins.
3. Create your tipping point.

1. Center yourself

Momentum requires preparation. The right place to start is with the jettison of the emotional baggage, the excuses, and even some of the responsibilities that weigh us down and create friction in our lives. Our objective is to make ourselves a little leaner and lighter in ways that we can control.

First, let go of your emotional baggage. It sounds simple, but most of us are unaware of the self-imposed limitations that we carry around. For example, one of the executives we interviewed told us about a realization she had. She was passed over for two consecutive promotions and she was ready to throw in the towel on her career. She was beginning to believe that she wasn't cut out to be a leader.

After some feedback from trusted friends and some coaching, she realized she was holding herself back. Eventually, she identified the root cause of her confidence deficit and was able to let go of the limitation. Whether it's a confidence issue, indecision, fear, or whatever, work to identify your internal barriers.

Next, say good-bye to convenient excuses. The tendency to make excuses to explain setbacks is another stubborn mind-set issue that can hold you back. Excuses don't weigh you down like emotional baggage does, but they send you off in the wrong direction. One way to lose your excuses is by honing an *aim frame* instead of a *blame frame*.[4] A blame frame mind-set "focuses on the problem and why it occurred."[5] It's about assigning blame. An aim frame mind-set goes straight to determining what next steps will most effectively make things right. An aim frame is about where you are going and how you are getting people to believe in you and go along with you. The aim frame mentality keeps you moving in a positive direction; a blame frame outlook stops you cold. Again, it is all about moving your energy forward.

Finally, let go of responsibilities that are not a part of your plan. As women, we multitask madly to keep lots of balls in the air. But it's not practical to say yes to planning the company holiday party and cochairing a school fund-raiser if your aim is to run an organization that keeps you busy, body and soul, for fifty-plus hours a week. It all comes down to your goals. Generating momentum requires letting go of the things that matter less to you. You must focus!

2. Generate a string of small wins

As we saw with Sapna, delivering on a string of meticulously planned interim successes can add up to something big. We're on board with that. In fact, we coach women to use the power of small wins to charge up their career momentum. Our process for using small wins has some guidelines that are all our own.

Plan the wins. In addition to delivering on your major benchmarks, plan your small wins carefully. Meticulous management of small wins keeps stakeholders engaged and on board while you make the bigger progress they are looking for. Pilot projects are a relatively safe way to accumulate small wins without betting the ranch.

Advertise and celebrate at multiple levels. The only way to build on small wins is to fully own them. When you exceed expectations, it's up to you to make sure people know about it. When Sapna could show that her pilot program was popular with customers, she not only presented the results to the board, she also encouraged colleagues who were involved in the program to share their stories of success with their peers. Before long, word got around and people were actively lobbying Sapna to expand the pilot.

Use meaningful specifics. The original sales guru Zig Ziglar says, "Don't become a 'wandering generality.' Be a 'meaningful specific.' "[6] Plan for small wins and focus on the deliverables that mean the most to your stakeholders. Sapna was right on the mark—lowering costs and elevating customer satisfaction was exactly what the organization was looking for. When we are asked about our projects, our tendency is to say, "The project is going well." Instead, try saying this:

"We saved $10,000 dollars."
"We improved customer satisfaction by 70 percent."
"We reduced cycle time by 15 percent."

Manage surprises. Save surprises for birthdays, not bosses and supporters. If you are sensing a setback on the horizon, start steering people toward a more realistic small win. The key is to avoid surprises, remain in control, and maintain the perception of ongoing success.

Small wins carve large, complex goals into manageable chunks. You'll find that these ta-da moments generate not only logistical momentum for your project or career but also a significant emotional lift that accelerates your pace and progress. Betty Thompson at Booz Allen Hamilton said, "Women need to be more deliberate." We agree.

What Stalls Momentum?

SURPRISES

- No one likes to be surprised—prepare people in advance.

- The "smell of bad news" gets worse over time. Announce setbacks early.

- Be transparent to depoliticize setbacks and crowdsource solutions.

LACK OF TRANSPARENCY

- If people think you are hiding something, it slows progress.

- Trust is a main building block of momentum.

UNCLEAR INTENT

- If your vision and objectives are unclear, your agenda won't get off the ground.

- Cathy Bessant, chief operations and technology officer at Bank of America, advised, "Be upfront and communicate your intention or people may be suspicious of your motives."

- Know your message. What is your *one-line* takeaway? Stay on point.

- Make sure others see themselves in your vision.

LACK OF STRATEGY

- Being purely tactical gets your to-do list completed but it will not take you to the top.

- Companies want people who can innovate, drive change, and transform.

3. Create your tipping point

Our final strategy for building momentum does so through followership. While the other strategic actions we've discussed will start to mobilize the critical mass you need, support from the people around you is what creates the tipping point that will sustain momentum and eventually deliver influence.

A *tipping point*, as described by author Malcolm Gladwell, is "the moment of critical mass, the threshold, the boiling point."[7] For our purposes, we use the metaphor of rolling the boulder uphill. Although the climb is hard work, the coalition of support we accumulate along the way gets us to the peak—and our momentum multiplies as the boulder rolls briskly down the other side.

Generating followership requires employing the strategies we described in the previous chapter for building relationships. It also requires the ability of a leader to articulate a vision that inspires people. At the beginning of this chapter, we told Denise's story. She had an idea that was innovative and important, but she was not able to get her executive colleagues to take the leap with her, so they shut her down. However, Denise regrouped. She repaired her relationships and began to build a *coalition* of support around her plan to create a platform for real-time sales results. She created a framework to measure progress, and she also articulated a dynamic vision that excited followers. This time Denise leveraged the groundswell of followership she developed. She got her sales platform launched, and it put her reputation back in a positive light. Her do-over (we love do-overs) created momentum for the project and for her career.

No matter what the specifics of your goal, followership and momentum are inextricably linked. None of us can roll that boulder all the way over the peak alone. Reginald Van Lee of Booz Allen Hamilton (retired) said, "You have to get things done in an environment where there are multiple agendas and different levels of power and control." We need energized supporters to speak and act on our behalf. We coach women that followership today comes from all corners of an organization—above, below, and across.

Neither followership nor momentum happens overnight, and there is no one path to take. Yet building followership as a path to momentum can help you reach a tipping point. Just as momentum and followership are linked, followership is closely connected to influence. The wave of support that followers provide generates momentum and opens a channel for influence to begin to develop.

* * *

The physics behind the Influence Effect is cumulative in nature. Small wins and followership generate momentum and energy. This energy leads to a greater lift toward your transformational vision.

Career Momentum: Move Sideways to Move Up

Gaining momentum doesn't always mean moving directly upward. Often, it simply means proceeding in a strategic direction to avoid halting all progress.

Two of the executives we coach are being sponsored by the chief information officer (CIO) of a large insurance company. One of us took the time recently to interview the CIO to hear about her circuitous career path. Prior to becoming CIO, she was an audit officer at the firm. Before that she was a compliance chief, a marketing executive, a unit manager, and even a risk management director—all at the same firm. Moving sideways to move up is a savvy way to build your reputation and gain career momentum on the path to a top leadership position. Companies like GE and Cisco are famous for moving their best and brightest around and giving them experience rotating through different roles. This type of "sideways momentum" is particularly important to women who have held senior-level roles in operations but have no frontline exposure or P&L responsibility. The benefits of a lateral rotation are numerous: It can dramatically boost your experience. It pressure tests you in new situations. It gets you out in front of senior leaders who may be able to sponsor your next promotion. You become known as someone who learns quickly and is fungible. In short, your stock price skyrockets.

Sideways momentum can also be a launchpad when your career is feeling stale or unfulfilling. In a 2016 survey of two thousand full-time American employees cited in *Harvard Business Review*, 89 percent of respondents said they would "consider making a lateral career move with no financial incentive" in order to achieve greater personal satisfaction or pursue a new career path.[8]

Lateral moves are not for everyone, and they depend on your current career trajectory. What matters is that you consider moving sideways instead of up when you are looking for ways to increase career momentum and satisfaction. This may mean moving in the direction of the "hot area"— toward great leaders whom you admire, to where the growth is going to occur, or to the areas where things need to be fixed and you could be a hero. One executive said, "Figure out who and what is rising and rise with them."

Executive Summary

- Momentum is most often halted by difficult political dynamics, extreme modesty, and a lack of clear strategic intent.
- Achieving momentum requires us to carefully manage our direction, perspective, and alignment.
- Momentum requires preparation. The right place to start is with the jettison of the baggage and excuses—and even some of the responsibilities that create friction in our lives.
- Small wins carve large, complex goals into manageable chunks. These ta-da moments generate logistical momentum for your agenda and a significant emotional lift that accelerates your pace and progress.
- Followership creates the tipping point that will sustain momentum and eventually deliver influence.
- Sideways momentum can be a launchpad when your career is feeling stale or unfulfilled.

PART THREE

INFLUENCE
in Action

9

Dance with Resistance

THE BIG FIVE STRATEGIES WE have explored in chapters 4 through 8 are at the heart of the Influence Effect: *the power of the informal, relationship maps, scenario thinking, influence loops,* and *momentum.* These versatile tools deliver the type of influence and outcomes that women want. Cumulatively, they feed the creativity and confidence we need to lead at high levels in business. Separately, they provide us with the options and flexibility to address a multitude of situations in ways that work for us.

The following two chapters bring these ideas together, using common situations to show where women have the greatest opportunities to influence. You will notice that the format here is not identical to that in the strategy chapters, because our goal is to focus on examining the strategies in action. In chapter 10, "Meetings: A Case in Point," we look at achieving influence in business meetings. In this chapter, we will explore how to use these strategies to win over blockers and overcome rigid resistance to our ideas.

Findings from our 2013 research first pointed us to these topics. Part of what we found was that men and women perceive *conflict* differently. Men described "debate and competition" in these situations, whereas women described "confrontation and conflict." Men said they felt that women "lost their composure" faster than men when they were met with a head-on challenge or a direct rebuke.

One female vice president said this: "When men dismiss women, women interpret it as being 'put in our place,' and it's frustrating. We don't like the conflict and we don't know how to come back in a way that does not appear defensive."

Most of the women in our 2013 study were senior-level female executives in male-dominated organizations and industries. We believe that these women were "defensive" and less comfortable in group conflicts in part because they were outnumbered by male colleagues.

An additional point of divergence was that women reported having a negative response to workplace conflict *in general*—even when they were not a party to it. Women said they found it unsettling when someone— anyone—received criticism or resistance, and they felt sympathy for the person. In this case, women talked about feeling empathy as opposed to feeling defensive.

Another relevant finding in our 2013 research was that women and men *use emotion differently* in conflict situations. The women believed they use emotion in the correct measure, whereas the men in the study said they wished women would use it less frequently and more strategically. Even more interestingly, *men and women disagreed about what emotion looks and sounds like*. In our review of 360-degree feedback surveys, we learned that when women say they feel "passionate" about an idea, their passion is sometimes misinterpreted by male managers and colleagues as "emotional."

Despite the differences, both male and female executives we interviewed were quick to point out that women get much less latitude than men when expressing emotion. As one male executive at JPMorgan Chase told us, "There is a fair amount of sensitivity about a woman losing her cool. If a man loses his cool and gets emotional or angry it's okay. But when a woman does, everyone's antennae are raised high and you can feel the tension."

What this indicates is that we, as women, are dealing with a double standard at the same time that we are in the midst of a conflict situation. Conflicts occur routinely in all professional settings. It is our hope, then, that the strategies presented throughout this book enable us women to be ourselves, leverage our strengths, and pass the many political tests we experience along the path to achieving influence.

We find ourselves on calls every day with the women we coach, helping them navigate conflicts and negotiate with critics using the strategies presented here. While some of these "resisters" are colleagues who simply see things differently, others are individuals with opposing agendas and competing interests who see business as a zero-sum game. Regardless, the women we know who are most successful use numerous tools to build influence. One of the executives we coach managed a difficult situation beautifully, and it offers lessons that all of us can learn from. It was a particularly sticky dilemma because her blocker was the company's chief financial officer (CFO), who was trying to make a show of strength in front of his boss—the new CEO.

> *Liz is a senior vice president who leads a large marketing department at a regional bank. By 2014, the U.S. banking sector had largely recovered from the recession of 2008–2009. Still, there was considerable caution, and the bank was preparing to conduct a round of layoffs. The action came down from the new CEO, who earnestly wanted to "right-size the teams to suit the current scope of business."*
>
> *Liz was on board and she worked with the CFO, Colin, and Michael, the senior vice president of operations, to determine how many people she would need to release from her unit. Beyond acting with fairness toward those who would be affected by the layoffs, Liz's primary objective was to keep as many staff members as she could. She wanted her teams to achieve their business goals for the year, and that meant not putting immediate cost cutting above longer-term results.*
>
> *Just days before the layoffs were scheduled to be carried out, one of Liz's senior marketing managers handed in her notice. This individual was an outstanding performer, and she wasn't on the list to be displaced. Bingo: Liz saw an opening. She went straight to Colin and made the case to keep a marketing manager to backfill the open position.*

Colin flatly refused. "No way," he told her. "We're finalizing the severance packages with HR and I just ran everything by Gene [the CEO]. Nothing changes!"

Liz wasn't ready to let it go. She stopped in to see one of her longtime supporters in HR. When she asked if it was indeed too late to pull a package out of her stack, he replied, "It wouldn't be a problem. We can pull it out any time until we hand them out."

She went back to Colin, this time to make the case that she would be able to meet her budget projections for the year if she kept this particular slot filled. She also mentioned that HR would be fine with the switch. According to Liz, Colin was irritated at her for "going around him" to consult with HR. She let him vent for a few minutes and then said, "Colin, you can meet your budget and keep one more person from losing their job. It's the right thing to do, however, I will support your decision."

After her conversation with Colin, Liz updated Michael, who was managing the logistics of the downsizing. Michael was a close friend of Colin's and he knew the specifics of how Liz's unit operated and the role her senior marketing managers played. She asked Michael for his support.

On the day before they were scheduled to announce the layoffs, Colin strode into Liz's office and sat down. "Okay, you can take a name off the list." He did not explain why he had changed his mind, and Liz didn't ask. She simply said, "Good decision, Colin!"

Liz maneuvered through this politically fraught situation. Her subtle moves and astute responses illustrate what we mean by *dancing with resistance*. Liz needed to "dip and twirl" a bit to reach her objective. It required several rounds and approaches to influence the outcome. She was being responsive and assertive at the same time. And she was confident enough to take a few calculated risks. Although it's not always smart to route around the top boss, Liz saw a clear opening and used it to get everyone dancing to the same song. Let's take a closer look at the guiding principles she used to achieve influence over the outcome in this situation.

THREE QUESTIONS to Deal with Resisters

Liz made her win look easy, but it was carefully orchestrated. We know because we were coaching her at the time. Her strategy was guided by three key questions that should be part of any campaign to bypass resistance and beat blockers.

1. What is this disagreement really about?

Pause to identify the particulars of this disagreement. Why is this person resisting you? What does the person have to gain? What does he or she have to lose? What extenuating circumstances are at play?

Liz asked around and pieced together what was happening below the surface of the situation. Colin was indeed making a power play... but not against Liz. His resistance, she thought, was a way to look good in front of his new boss—the CEO who called for the layoffs. Liz knew that both men were extremely concerned about financial results for the year. She made it known that exempting the marketing manager's job would not have a negative impact on financial results and Colin would meet his layoff goal.

2. What is the power dynamic?

Power is a tricky word for women. Many of us perceive it in a negative light. However, different types of power are at play whenever human beings are in conflict. In business settings, power is most commonly delivered from one's *position in the hierarchy*, one's *level of expertise*, or both. If your resister is a *peer*, you are probably on level ground with him or her politically—which indicates that you have some latitude in terms of how to proceed. It also means that you can pause to put yourself in their place and ask yourself, what would I do if I were them? Quid pro quo deal making is one common way to manage a peer resister—but there are other effective ways, such as using influence loops to overcome their resistance.

If your resister is a *member of a team you manage,* you usually have the upper hand where power is concerned. And yet, team members need to be managed very gingerly. They can gain the upper hand fast if they are perceived to be the victim in a power struggle with a superior. In addition, they are in a prime position to damage your reputation should they bad-mouth you to other colleagues. Proceed with caution and never underestimate team members who are bold enough to block a boss.

If your resister has more power than you, then your options are more limited and your success depends on highly astute political maneuvering. This was the position Liz found herself in. Her resister was a C-suite executive, and she acted with that in mind. On the one hand, she was respectful and made it clear that he would make the final decision. On the other hand, she did not feel the need to treat him with kid gloves. She leveraged her relationships with peers in HR and operations, and they acted on her behalf behind the scenes.

3. Has trust been established?

How do you feel about your resister and his or her motives? Do you trust the person? Does he or she trust you? This was an easy one for Liz. She had known Colin for years and she trusted him. She believed that he trusted her. This led Liz to believe that Colin wanted to do the right thing. In the end, she gave him a way to do exactly that.

A Quick Reference Guide: Common Scenarios for Resisters

It can be difficult to get into the mind of a resister, but it is imperative to do so. You must understand their motives in order to win them over or neutralize their objections. Here is a list of the most common scenarios we hear about from our clients.

Reasons That Bosses Become Resisters

- "I have failed to make a convincing case to him for my idea or plan."

- "I have not earned her trust."

- "My boss just does not support women."

- "He has a personal agenda and will not go out of his way to help me."

Reasons That Peers Become Resisters

- "She and I are competing for limited resources."

- "I have to get my project done, but I have no authority over my peers."

- "He wants my job."

- "We just don't get along. He doesn't want to support me."

- "There is ambiguous accountability and she and I are getting in each other's way."

Reasons That Team Members Become Resisters

- "I was promoted over them."

- "He wants to undermine my authority."

- "She is upset because I did not promote her."

STRATEGIES for Neutralizing Resisters

Resisters emerge from high up in organizations, from the ground floor, and from everywhere in between, and they withhold support or directly oppose you for numerous reasons. The trio of questions we used with Liz will help guide you in planning a strategy to win over or go around resisters. Let's also look at several of the influence strategies presented in previous chapters to examine how they can be used.

Build trust before you need it

Many of the strategies in this chapter, and throughout this book, are aimed at moving toward your competitors, adversaries, or resisters as opposed to keeping your distance and turning away. This is because building influence requires generating trust. After all, most opposition occurs due to a lack of trust. As we said in chapter 7, building trust *before* you need it keeps your resisters to a minimum. As the inevitable naysayers emerge, always ask yourself, how can I establish trust? You either need to use trust to forge a path that is big enough for the both of you or enlist enough support to simply plow ahead. Regardless, trust is the key to influence, and it is also at the center of our dance with resistance.

Use facts to persuade

When you encounter resistance, go find the facts. Does your plan *improve cycle time by 20 percent?* Do the numbers prove that it will *reduce costs and elevate efficiencies?* The wonderful thing about facts is that they require very little interpretation. Facts speak for themselves, and they are an indispensable part of any persuasion campaign. A rule of thumb is to do your homework and have three to five facts at your fingertips that help strengthen your case and make your position harder to block. This dovetails nicely with the idea of using meaningful specifics, as mentioned in chapter 8. Facts and figures are a type of meaningful specific that can quantify the upside of your idea and lend rigor to your agenda.

Align your goals with theirs

Finding common goals is an excellent way to turn blockers into allies and resisters into supporters. To flip the dynamic in this way, influencers need to know more than *why* a blocker is opposing their plan. They also need to know what the blocker wants instead. Oftentimes, there is ample overlap hidden within opposing arguments. Finding alignment requires changing one's perspective. For instance, when your team wants to grow by acquiring a Seattle-based vendor and your blocker wants to merge with a company in Singapore, begin by focusing on a merger instead of the specific partner. No matter how vast your differences are, identifying your commonalities will bring you closer together.

Interestingly, individuals might not even realize they agree with you until you point out the commonalities that exist between your perspectives. Taking the time to communicate common ground is a positive, effective way to win allies and influence an outcome. No matter how you approach it, common ground works for women because it enables us to achieve our objectives in a win-win way.

Rethink your communication approach

When an idea you have floated goes over like a lead balloon, don't necessarily scrap the notion altogether; just tweak how you talk about it. We've seen this seldom-used strategy work wonders in winning over supporters.[1] The trick is to focus on three crucial factors. First, know your audience. Your elevator speech should be tailored for each audience. A pitch that appeals to customers, for example, won't contain the same nuggets as one that engages a board member. Next, figure out *why* you are being blocked. Understanding the opposing argument will strengthen your message and help bring blockers on board. Finally, take the direct approach and open a line of communication with the opposition. Many times, resistant people get locked into an entrenched stance and dialogue is what finally draws them out. Ask, "How would it be possible for you to support this?" This transformational question alters the conversation from a "yes but" exchange to one in which you are discussing the possibilities and finally getting to yes. The direct approach stimulates creative thinking and can turn a deadlock into a collaborative effort.

Turn to your tribe

Some resisters seem like they may *never* yield their position, and perhaps they never will. They might be holding a grudge or competing against you for resources. What's your plan? When women try everything to turn around their blockers and come up short, we tell them to forget about the resisters and focus on building support. Remain positive and call on your agents, sponsors, and followers to work on your behalf.

How you utilize your support depends on who the resister is. If your blocker is your boss, start by asking a well-placed sponsor to make your case when the time is right. If your blocker is a peer, a groundswell of followers can often turn the tide in your favor. Regardless, a strong show of support has a multiplier effect that can win over (or wear down) blockers with time.

Pick your battles

Sometimes the simplest strategies pack a real punch. Several of the executives we interviewed insisted that the best influencers always know how to choose their battles. Here's what they said:

- "They know when a battle is worth the political capital it will require to win."
- "They take the time to evaluate the situation. And they have a framework to help them decide when to stand their ground and when to gracefully fold."
- "They know that resistance cannot always be overcome. Sometimes they pack it in and live to fight another day."

What all this means is that we must be strategic in deciding if our broader interests are best served by digging in or by compromising on our position and perhaps gaining supporters in the process.

To get a lift from the Influence Effect, you have to figure out how to deal with individuals who do not support your ideas. You are going to experience resistance—it's just a matter of when—so carefully plan how you will smoothly navigate it.

Executive Summary

- Naming the power dynamic that is at play helps us identify our options and isolate our limitations in a resistance situation.
- Know the specifics: Why is this person resisting? What does the person have to gain? What does he or she have to lose? What extenuating circumstances are at play?
- It can be difficult to get inside the mind of a resister, but it is imperative to do so. We must understand resisters' motives in order to win them over or neutralize their objections.
- Trust is the key to influence. We must ask ourselves, How do I feel about my resister and his or her motives? Do I trust the person? Does he or she trust me?
- We can win over resisters by generating trust, leading with facts, aligning our goals with those of the resisters, altering our communication style, turning to our tribe, and picking our battles.

10

Meetings:
A Case in Point

D URING AN EXECUTIVE PLANNING MEETING, one executive among twenty around a large conference table received a text message. It was from a colleague sitting just a few chairs away. It read, "Say something right now. Make sure your voice is heard. Ask a question." Later, the executive learned that the CEO was planning to shrink the size of the committee. There was a concern that a few of the individuals in the room were not contributing enough to make the cut.[1]

Another senior leader, fifteen years into a successful career as a marketing executive, had a similar experience. The executive, generally considered by peers to be assertive and insightful, was surprised when a colleague stopped by after a meeting to deliver some stern advice: "Stop acting like a facilitator. Start saying what you stand for: What is your point of view?"

Finally, a division leader managing a $50 million business unit, who, according to performance feedback, was widely admired and respected, had the same type of wake-up call. After failing to contribute in senior manager meetings because "you need to shout to be heard," colleagues said the executive's silence in strategic discussions was one reason this person had not been promoted into a senior leadership role.

These three executives have a few things in common. First, they are all successful. They are ambitious and motivated to take their careers to the next level. Second, they are all well liked by colleagues and superiors, yet they have been dinged repeatedly for a lack of engagement, lack of powerful behavior, and lack of visibility in meetings. Finally—as you might have guessed—all three of these executives are women.

Our research tells us that these stories are quite common. In our study from 2013 that canvassed male and female senior executives, 46 percent of the women we surveyed said they have significant difficulty inserting themselves into key meeting discussions. Likewise, a full 50 percent of men said the most important thing women should address in meeting settings is being more confident and direct and less equivocal and apologetic.

This topic of effectively wielding influence in business meetings is relevant for several reasons. First, meetings—whether in person, by videoconference, or by conference call—are the "center stage" at corporations. Meetings allow executives to showcase their ideas and contributions and take part in key decisions about the business. Given that many women report feeling stuck in midlevel positions, this idea of meetings as public forums becomes highly relevant. Meetings afford a direct line to senior decision makers and a seat at the table, thereby leveling the playing field in terms of access. Also, the higher up you go, the more time you spend in meetings. You must get good at it. Given the import of meetings and the high likelihood of political dynamics therein, what better place to drill down?

The meeting setting is an ideal venue for examining the behaviors and strategies that we can apply in our ongoing quest to achieve influence.

WHY MEETINGS MATTER More for Women

Meetings represent a crucial opportunity for all leaders. Why? Because they are the main venue in which business reputations are made and lost. This is especially true for women executives. When we are minorities in the top tiers of business, our every move draws critical attention that either opens doors or holds us back. Simply put, at this point in time, women have more on the line in these high-stakes interactions than male counterparts.

Meetings can open doors for women. In the initial ten to fifteen years after entering the workforce, most employees rise in their careers based on the merits of their individual contributions. After that, the fortunes of senior-level women executives accelerate or stagnate based on two altogether different metrics. The first is the financial performance of their unit. This is to be expected, and it is the same for both male and female leaders. The second factor is more interesting—it is the ability of a woman leader to gain the active sponsorship of at least one C-suite executive. We have seen that a major way to gain that sponsorship is to perform well in meetings.

This theme of women struggling to have our voices acknowledged in meetings is not entirely new. Yet, beyond this larger theme, we have isolated two important findings that took us by surprise. Our first finding, over the course of our yearlong research study, was that even women at the very highest levels stepped up to corroborate the extent of the problem.

Beginning in 2012 we examined over seven thousand 360-degree feedback surveys on 1,100 high-ranking female executives working at the level of vice president or above. We found that meetings were a clear stumbling block, regardless of rank and job title. In 2013 we surveyed 270 female managers in Fortune 500 organizations, including McDonald's, Procter & Gamble, and Walmart. Over half of the respondents reported that meetings were a significant issue for them or a "work in progress." Lastly, we went on to interview 65 top executives, both male and female, including CEOs, not only to get a gut check on our findings but also to hear their own experiences. We coded the responses from each executive to identify themes that represent a dominant perspective. These leaders, from JPMorgan Chase, Deloitte, PepsiCo, Lowe's, Time Warner, eBay, and several other organizations, helped us piece together the specifics of the gender divide in meetings.

What we found is that women executives, vastly outnumbered in boardrooms and executive suites, with fewer role models and sponsors to bring them into what still often amounts to a private club, can feel alone and outside their comfort zones in some high-level meetings. As one of only a few women in the room, they also frequently reported feeling unsupported and less able to advocate forcefully for their ideas and perspectives. As one female executive said, "It is harder to read the room if there are no other women around the table."

Regardless of why this problem persists, coming across as powerful and persuasive in meetings is a critical issue for women. Given the differences in how men and women describe the problem, it is clear that a part of this dilemma is perception. Perception is always an issue when gender politics comes into play. Still, the fact remains that success in visible forums such as meetings is a part of what gets people promoted. Even beyond career success, meetings, from the board level on down, are where decisions are made. Women must have the tools they need to be at their best and achieve the influence they want and deserve.

MEETINGS MATTER: A Checklist for Being Your Best

☐ Know the real purpose of the meeting.

☐ Be strategic: decide in advance how you need to "show up" (be perceived) at the meeting.

☐ Be prepared to ask questions that take the meeting to a new level.

☐ Remain on an even keel: perception matters.

☐ Let it go. Avoid post-meeting angst.

RAVE REVIEWS on the Corporate Stage

Attributes that land us in executive roles—such as ambition, experience, intelligence, and talent—are only part of what we need to become influential leaders. Alongside these core competencies are others that help us become more effective and successful. Let's review strategies and behaviors that deliver influence for women in meetings.

Be intentional

Because so many different dynamics are at play, we coach women to walk into the meeting with a clear plan for themselves.

This requires thinking about how you want to be perceived. Generally, you want others to "experience" you and get the impression that you are fully engaged and knowledgeable. You want to be seen as confident and creative. Whatever your objective, know the impression you want to impart and plan to project it.

As one female executive in Silicon Valley told us, knowing what impression you want to make can help you plan every facet of how you act at a meeting: "how to walk in, what to wear, where to sit, when to talk, and how to respond."

Similarly, we coach women to think of themselves as a brand. Before attending an important meeting, be intentional about your image and messaging. This may be an opportunity to prove yourself to a prospective sponsor or raise your profile with peers. Regardless, simply take a few moments to consider your goals and prepare yourself.

Have a point of view

Being intentional also applies to the content you bring into a meeting. Come in with a clear understanding of what the team is trying to accomplish and how it dovetails with your own agenda. Most important, be prepared to share and defend your unique point of view.

We coach women to consider the content of the discussion and engage the group with three things in mind. First, decide in advance what one or two things you want to accomplish and what key points will help you get there. Next, be concise and inject value by adding your own relevant perspective. Share something relevant that brings the conversation to the next level instead of seconding what the previous person had to say. Finally, stand ready to own your point of view and sell your ideas.

Having a strong, distinct perspective will enhance your reputation and enable you to sell your ideas and make the meeting better.

Use amplification

In the beginning of Barack Obama's first term in office, about two-thirds of the top White House staffers were men who had worked on the campaign. The female aides were outnumbered and being shut out of important meetings. When they did make it into meetings, their ideas were either being drowned out or hijacked. "It's not pleasant to have to appeal to a man to say, 'Include me in that meeting,'" National Security Adviser Susan Rice told the *Washington Post*, explaining how women in the Obama administration sometimes had to lobby to be included in key discussions.[2]

Rice and her female colleagues solved their dilemma by adopting a strategy they called "amplification." When a woman in their group made a key point, another woman in the room would repeat it, giving credit to its author. This simple tactic forced the men in the room to acknowledge the first woman's contribution—and denied them the chance to co-opt the idea and claim it as their own.

This is a strategy that any of us can use in meetings—and many of our coaching clients *have* used it with great success. Looking to other women for support, and supporting them back, is empowering and helps us create and solidify a coalition of like-minded female allies.

Get your voice in the room

Are you an introvert who struggles to muster the confidence to get your voice in the room? Having worked with many women who share your anxiety, we designed some simple advice to make speaking up easier:

Arrive early. Getting into the room early and choosing your seat helps you to get acclimated to the environment. It also positions you to acknowledge people as they enter and creates an initial rapport that will make you more comfortable.

Speak early. Getting your voice in the room early sends the message that you are there to participate. It also gets you warmed up and positions you as part of the dialogue before the conversation gets commandeered by the usual suspects.

Ask a question. Something as simple as a question may be enough to cement your place in the discussion. One woman we coach told us that she has the most impact in meetings when she finds an opportunity "to turn the meeting in a different and more productive direction by posing insightful questions. Have you thought of this...? Or, What if we looked at it this way...?" Questions start a type of dialogue that can be transformative.

Getting your voice in the room with a pertinent point makes an impression. Better still, it gets easier. Once you have a system in place, speaking up in meetings becomes second nature.

Be concise and use muscular language

In executive settings, the discussion can move so quickly it becomes tricky even to get a word in. Conversations, like tennis, move from point to point and players need to be prepared when it is their turn to serve and volley. One smart way to win is simply by using speech to convey power. Being concise and on point can give you the edge you need to get your opinion heard.

Another way to get into the conversation is by using "muscular" words that are authoritative and direct. Instead of saying, "How about this …," say, "I strongly suggest…." Or, instead of saying, "Maybe we can…," say, "Here is my plan…."

If this type of executive discourse does not come naturally to you, put in some practice time. Rehearse while you are driving to work or use your smartphone to record yourself speaking. Plan your opening remarks or key argument. Lynne Ford, executive vice president, division executive, private wealth at SunTrust told us, "You need to have written down some things you want to talk about. Even some of the casual remarks you hear have been rehearsed. If it sounds good, it was probably prepared."

Do the meeting before the meeting

Most of the men in our study, and many women, said that the "meeting before the meeting" is where the real work happens. In the days, hours, or minutes before a meeting, connect with colleagues to test your ideas and get an indication of support. These conversations are informal and can occur in passing: in the hallway, in the elevator, or on the walk to the train. Being fully prepared for a meeting means never asking a question when you do not already know the answer.

According to a male senior vice president, "Men are really good at the pre-meeting. They go by the office to talk, throw the ball to each other almost in a conversation, and they work their agenda for the meeting. This pre-meeting behavior enables them to be successful because they've mustered support for their ideas. This is their preparation. It happens before anyone gets to the table and it's very important."

The pre-meeting has multiple benefits: it allows individuals to increase their familiarity with the issues, vet ideas, canvass for votes, and refine their points of view. Taking part in the informal conversations that happen in advance also helps women identify the real purpose of the meeting. Frequently, the actual rationale is not reflected in the written agenda. Is the meeting being called to establish a consensus? Solve a problem? The purpose of a meeting may also be somewhat subjective, depending on the politics of the group. Regardless, the meeting before the meeting will help to clarify any distinction between the stated and actual purpose of the meeting.

In addition, it is important to realize that key issues are often fully resolved in pre-meeting discussions, before the real meeting even starts. As one male executive told us, "The decisions are made in advance and some women don't seem to know it." This leaves us out of the decision making.

Don't take it personally

We coach women to know when to let it go when a meeting does not go their way. As one woman told us, "I need to refrain from taking business so personally." In addition, we found in our review of 360-degree feedback reports, and in our research, that women have a certain retained angst. That is, we second-guess ourselves after a meeting and replay events over and over instead of moving on. Regardless of the specific challenges, picking our shots (and remaining objective) helps all of us remain fully engaged in the meeting and making meaningful contributions.

* * *

Our rationale for offering these hands-on strategies is simple: it reinforces the idea that influence is something that all of us can learn and practice. Of course, our approach is seldom fixed. As when trying on clothes in a department store, we each need to choose the size and style that suits us.

There is one story from our recent experience that we think sums up what the Influence Effect looks like. It is about a woman one of us coached off and on for several years. In that time, we witnessed her personal transformation as she changed from a less-than-secure associate director with a bad case of impostor syndrome to someone who owns her success and has become one of the top three people at a global management consulting practice. Recently, when she got up to deliver the annual state-of-the-organization address in front of the entire company, the audience seemed to hang on her every word. People were smiling and nodding their heads, and they watched her without losing interest or looking down at their smartphones. She caught the "big wave" we talked about earlier and she had a great ride.

We talked to her later that afternoon and complimented her on the connection she had with the audience. She said that her secret came down to one word: trust.

"They trust you?" we asked.

She shook her head. "Yes, they do," she replied, "but what I mean is that *I trust myself.*"

All of her commitment to improvement and practice over the years helped her develop confidence, win support, and earn the influence that was so apparent to us in the annual address. We hope that you, too, will use these strategies as you grow as a leader and look for opportunities to have impact and achieve influence. It is our belief that the Influence Effect happens over time and has a cumulative effect. As you use these strategies to develop followership and lead the changes that you believe in, influence will emerge as both a by-product of your success and a driver of it. The Influence Effect will enable each of us to rise above office politics and achieve success on our own terms, not because the gender dynamics that we face no longer exist but because they no longer hold us back.

Executive Summary

- Still vastly outnumbered in boardrooms and executive suites, with fewer role models and sponsors to bring us into what amounts to a private club, many of us feel outside our comfort zones in some high-level meetings.
- As women, we are sometimes "out-muscled" by male colleagues who take up more space and power their way into the dialogue.
- We can bolster our perspective with concise facts, direct remarks, and "muscular language."
- Being intentional in how we present ourselves, articulating our point of view, and owning our ideas raises our profile in meetings.
- We can have our voices heard in the room by getting our points in early, remaining on topic, and amplifying each other's ideas.
- The "meeting before the meeting" allows us to increase our familiarity with the issues, vet ideas, canvass for votes, and refine our point of view. It is often where the real work occurs and decisions are made.
- Meetings are an ideal venue for us to line up sponsors, build followership, and achieve influence.

CONCLUSION

The Effect of Influence

*Most of us do not realize how much
power we have.*

—BUMPER STICKER

W E AS WOMEN HAVE SO much to gain—and nearly nothing to lose—
by using the powerful influence strategies in this book.

Beyond the cumulative benefits of empowering individual women, the Influence Effect can be a game changer for organizations. Study after study reinforces the idea that gender-diverse leadership teams result in higher profitability, greater innovation, and balanced risk taking. The evidence is simply overwhelming. This should act as an incentive for top leaders in organizations to take a hard look at the number of women represented on their leadership teams at every level. Where the percentage of women does not adequately represent their workforce and customers, they would do well to take steps to increase female representation. Best-in-class companies have metrics that track gender representation and turnover. These companies fund and support leadership programs expressly designed to develop women leaders. They match their high-potential female leaders with executive-level sponsors, and design programs to enable coaching. Finally, best-in-class companies hold their top leaders accountable for retaining, training, and promoting female executives within their organizations. These are the types of actions that help companies succeed and be their best.

When American businesses achieve our firm's long-standing goal of having women in *at least 30 percent* of the top leadership roles, our society will be a better place. Not just for women, or companies, or the economy, but for everyone.

Now, a final bit of encouragement.

One of the many things that the Influence Effect delivers for women is a sense of empowerment. Influence gets us in the game without asking us to sacrifice our values. Unlike politics, influence is not a zero-sum activity. We can be influential without taking influence away from someone else. Influence also fosters a sense of intellectual excitement. As we've seen throughout the book, the active pursuit of influence is a lifelong journey and it creates a path for career progress.

Remember when we asked you to think bigger and aim higher? Now is the time for you to choose a goal. Focus on that next big step forward in your career. Now, pick out two or three strategies from this book and get to work. Ask for support and feedback from your advisors and sponsors. Remember, you may not succeed in your first attempt. Use these strategies as an opportunity to develop your "influence muscles." You must continue to develop them to get better and be stronger. The practice of influence is an ongoing endeavor. Even when you reach the highest levels of leadership, you will continue to fine-tune your influence capabilities. There is always a next influence loop to make, more connections to establish, and new ideas to champion.

We have presented dozens of tools for you to use. Choose a few and get started. Our hope is that you will use the Influence Effect as you walk to the water's edge, seize the biggest wave you can find, and ride it to the top tier of your organization.

Strategies for Influence

The following is a summary of the strategies you can employ to achieve influence, as described in chapters 2–10 of *The Influence Effect*:

Chapter 2: Think Bigger, Aim Higher

- Nurture your vision.
- Check the weather.
- Train your brain.
- Cut the grass.
- Embrace your passion.

Chapter 3: Construct Your Scaffolding

- Create a personal board of directors.
- Manage your mentor/sponsor mix.
- Find an agent, truth teller, and personal supporter.
- Work your scaffolding.

Chapter 4: The Power of the Informal

- Make meaningless time meaningful.
- Hold the meeting before the meeting.
- Understand the informal norms.
- Do it your way.
- Talk the talk.

Chapter 5: Relationship Maps

- Begin with the end in mind.
- Draw a relationship map.
- Examine the culture.
- Establish common ground.
- Take action!

Chapter 6: Scenario Thinking

- Banish fear.
- Determine your outcome.
- Create your options.
- Identify and assess your stakeholders.
- Respond to your constraints.
- Remain nimble and proceed.

Chapter 7: Influence Loops

- Build trust before you need it.
- Identify key stakeholders.
- Prepare yourself.
- Have face-to-face meetings.
- Repeat!
- Use the gift of the gap.

Chapter 8: Momentum

- Center yourself.
- Generate a string of small wins.
- Create your tipping point.

Chapter 9: Dance with Resistance

- Build trust before you need it.
- Use facts to persuade.
- Align your goals with theirs.
- Rethink your communication approach.
- Turn to your tribe.
- Pick your battles.

Chapter 10: Meetings: A Case in Point

- Be intentional.
- Have a point of view.
- Use amplification.
- Get your voice in the room.
- Be concise and use muscular language.
- Do the meeting before the meeting.
- Don't take it personally.

Methodology

The premises and data in this book are based on (1) our 2015–16 "Gender Perceptions of Office Politics" survey; (2) follow-up interviews with forty-four executives; and (3) an analysis of our database of 360-degree feedback reports.

1. "Gender Perceptions of Office Politics" Survey

Summary of the Survey

Do gender differences exist in the following areas?

- Description of office politics
- Like or dislike of office politics
- Perceived competency in political maneuvering
- The importance of political skills in relation to career success or advancement
- Perceptions of gender differences in corporate politics and political maneuvering
- How often women and men engage in office politics

Summary of the Findings

- Respondents in this study generally had a negative view of office politics.
- Respondents generally viewed office politics as difficult or time consuming.
- Respondents generally had high perceptions of their political maneuvering skills.
- Although both genders viewed political skills as important, females tended to agree more strongly that political skills are essential to their career-related success.
- Although both genders acknowledge that gender differences exist in the realm of office politics, women feel more strongly about them than men do.
- Women were more likely than men to indicate agreement with the assertion that men are better than women at political maneuvering.

- Women in this study reported that they engage in office politics more often than did men in this study.

Participants

- In total, there were 134 survey participants, including 87 females and 47 males in America. Of these participants,
    - 20.7 percent of the women and 29.8 percent of the men were in the C-suite;
    - 57.5 percent of the women and 46.8 percent of the men were at the executive level;
    - 13 percent of the women and 8 percent of the men were in middle management;
    - 6 percent of the women and 3 percent of the men were entrepreneurs or individual contributors.
- Participants were executives at companies including Duke Energy, Deloitte, Razorfish Health, Calvert Investments, Ingersoll Rand, Booz Allen Hamilton, American Express, Carolinas HealthCare System, Leidos, AIG, Bank of America, Fifth Third Bank, IBM, Jones Lang LaSalle, and Wells Fargo.

Analysis Procedure

- Chi-square tests were used to assess differences by gender.
- The chi-square determines whether we can conclude with 95 percent confidence that there is a relationship between participants' gender and their responses to the survey questions.

2. Additional Research

We conducted in-depth phone interviews with forty-four executive-level men and women in American corporations.

3. Database Analysis

We utilized our proprietary database of 7,500 360-degree feedback reports on top women executives in America.

Notes

Introduction

[1] All of the examples in this book are based on stories from the women we coach. Almost all names and places have been changed. If requested by the individual, story details are further masked.

[2] Kathryn Heath, Jill Flynn, and Mary Davis Holt, "Women, Find Your Voice," *Harvard Business Review,* June 2014, https://hbr.org/2014/06/women-find-your-voice.

[3] Justin Wolfers, "When Teamwork Doesn't Work," *New York Times,* January 8, 2016, http://www.nytimes.com/2016/01/10/upshot/when-teamwork-doesnt-work-for-women.html?emc=eta1.

Chapter 1

Epigraph: The managing editor of *Time,* Nancy Gibbs, said this in 2014 about the magazine's "Time 100" list of influential people, published Friday, April 25, 2014. https://en.wikipedia.org/wiki/Time_100#cite_note-6. Accessed June 28, 2017.

[1] "Women CEOs of the S&P 500," Catalyst, April 25, 2017, http://www.catalyst.org/knowledge/women-ceos-sp-500.

[2] "Pyramid: Women in S&P 500 Companies," Catalyst, March 1, 2017, http://www.catalyst.org/knowledge/women-sp-500-companies.

[3] Gillian Tett, "The Dearth of Women in the Tech World Is Cultural and Therefore Entirely Reversible," *Chicago Tribune,* March 20, 2017, http://www.chicagotribune.com/news/sns-wp-tech-comment-8b1716f0-0d7e-11e7-9d5a-a83e627dc120-20170320-story.html.

[4] Elena Kvochko, "Why There Are Still Few Women Leaders in Tech," *Forbes,* January 4, 2016, https://www.forbes.com/sites/elenakvochko/2016/01/04/women-executives-in-tech/#6317ea1155e7.

[5] "Quick Take: Women in Academia," Catalyst, July 9, 2015, http://www.catalyst.org/knowledge/women-academia.

Chapter 2

Epigraph: Mary Oliver, *New and Selected Poems* (Boston: Beacon Press, 1992), 94.

[1] Herminia Ibarra and Otilia Obodaru, "Women and the Vision Thing," *Harvard Business Review,* January 2009, https://hbr.org/2009/01/women-and-the-vision-thing.

[2] Liz Ryan, "How to Explain Why You Left a Toxic Workplace," *Forbes,* October 18, 2016, http://www.forbes.com/sites/lizryan/2016/10/18/how-to-explain-why-you-left-a-toxic-workplace/#1a3803548bf3.

[3]Pauline Rose Clance and Suzanne Ament Imes, "The Imposter Phenomenon in High Achieving Women: Dynamics and Therapeutic Intervention," *Psychotherapy Theory, Research and Practice* 15, no. 3 (1978): 241–47.

[4]Susan Pinker, *The Sexual Paradox: Troubled Boys, Gifted Girls and the Real Difference between the Sexes* (New York: Scribner, 2008), 184–96.

[5]Satoshi Kanazawa and Kaja Perina, "Why Do So Many Women Experience the 'Imposter Syndrome'?" *Scientific Fundamentalist* (blog), December 13, 2009, http://www.psychologytoday.com/blog/the-scientific-fundamentalist/200912/why-do-so-many-women-experience-the-imposter-syndrome.

[6]Ibid.

Chapter 3

Epigraph: This lyrical adage is an often referenced Kenyan proverb.

[1]"Pyramid: Women in S&P 500 Companies," Catalyst, March 1, 2017, http://www.catalyst.org/knowledge/women-sp-500-companies.

[2]LeanIn.org and McKinsey, *Women in the Workplace, 2016*, extract, September 2016, http://www.mckinsey.com/business-functions/organization/our-insights/women-in-the-workplace-2016.

[3]Sylvia Ann Hewlett, "Constructing Your Career Castle," *Harvard Business Review*, August 27, 2013, https://hbr.org/2013/08/constructing-your-career-castl.

[4]Diane Reay, "Spice Girls, 'Nice Girls', 'Girlies' and Tomboys: Gender Discourses, Girls' Cultures and Femininities in the Primary Classroom," *Gender and Education* 13, no. 2 (2001): 153–66.

[5]Rachel Croson and Uri Gneezy, "Gender Differences in Preferences," *Journal of Economic Literature* 47, no. 2 (June 2009): 448–74.

[6]Herminia Ibarra, "Women Are Over-Mentored (but Under-Sponsored)," interview by Julia Kirby, HBR IdeaCast, August 2010, https://hbr.org/2010/08/women-are-over-mentored-but-un.

[7]Herminia Ibarra, Nancy M. Carter, and Christine Silva, "Why Men Still Get More Promotions than Women," *Harvard Business Review*, September 2010, https://hbr.org/2010/09/why-men-still-get-more-promotions-than-women?referral=00134.

[8]Sylvia Ann Hewlett, "The Right Way to Find a Career Sponsor," *Harvard Business Review*, September 11, 2013, https://hbr.org/2013/09/the-right-way-to-find-a-career-sponsor.

[9]Sylvia Ann Hewlett, *Forget a Mentor, Find a Sponsor: The New Way to Fast-Track Your Career* (Boston: Harvard Business Review Press, 2013).

Chapter 4

Epigraph: Rob Cross and Robert J. Thomas, "A Smarter Way to Network," *Harvard Business Review*, July–August 2011, https://hbr.org/2011/07/managing-yourself-a-smarter-way-to-network.

[1]"Invest in Golf," *Barron's*, March 30, 1998, cover.

[2]Carol Bartz and Lisa Lambert, "Why Women Should Do Less and Network More," *Fortune*, November 11, 2014, http://fortune.com/2014/11/12/why-women-should-do-less-and-network-more/.

Chapter 5

Epigraph: Scott Stratten and Allison Kramer, *UnMarketing: Stop Marketing. Start Engaging*, 2nd ed. (New York: Wiley, 2016).

[1]Deborah Tannen, *He Said, She Said: Instructor's Package* (Los Angeles: Into the Classroom Media, n.d.), 4, http://www.evgonline.com/Downloads/Hesaidshesaidinstr.guide.pdf.

[2]Marshall Goldsmith, *What Got You Here Won't Get You There: How Successful People Become Even More Successful* (New York: Hachette Books, 2007).

[3]Linda Babcock and Sara Laschever, "Interesting Statistics," website for *Women Don't Ask: Negotiation and the Gender Divide* (book), accessed May 1, 2017, http://www.womendontask.com/stats.html.

[4]Stephen R. Covey, *The 7 Habits of Highly Effective People Personal Workbook* (New York: Touchstone, 2004), 74.

Chapter 6

Epigraph: Maureen Orth, "Angela's Assets," *Vanity Fair*, accessed January 28, 2017, http://www.vanityfair.com/news/2015/01/angela-merkel-profile.

[1]Roger Martin, *The Opposable Mind* (Boston: Harvard Business School Press, 2007), 7.

[2]Ibid.

Chapter 7

Epigraph: Karen Dahut, executive vice president at Booz Allen Hamilton, told us this directly as part of our interview and survey research for this book.

[1]Dave Kurlan, "Who Are Better Salespeople—Men or Women?," *Understanding the Sales Force* (blog), October 22, 2008, http://www.omghub.com/salesdevelopmentblog/tabid/5809/bid/7054/Who-Are-Better-Salespeople-Men-or-Women.aspx.

[2]Jon Katzenbach, Ilona Steffen, and Caroline Kronley, "Culture Change That Sticks," *Harvard Business Review*, July–August 2012, https://hbr.org/2012/07/cultural-change-that-sticks.

[3]Peter Block, *The Empowered Manager: Positive Political Skills at Work* (San Francisco: Jossey-Bass, 1987).

Chapter 8

Epigraph: John C. Maxwell, *The 21 Irrefutable Laws of Leadership: Follow Them and People Will Follow You*, rev. ed. (Nashville: Thomas Nelson, 2007).

[1]*Cambridge Academic Content Dictionary*, s.v. "momentum," http://dictionary.cambridge.org/us/dictionary/english/momentum?q=Momentum.

[2]Jeanine Prime, *Women "Take Care," Men "Take Charge": Stereotyping of U.S. Business Leaders Exposed* (New York: Catalyst, 2005), 1, http://www.catalyst.org/system/files/Women_Take_Care_Men _Take_Charge_Stereotyping_of_U.S._Business_Leaders_Exposed.pdf.

[3]Katy Winter, "Secret to Success? Become a Boaster!," *Daily Mail*, January 14, 2014, http://www .dailymail.co.uk/femail/article-2539247/Women-feel-modest-holds-work-place.html.

[4]Lisa J. Marshall and Lucy D. Freedman, *Smart Work: The Syntax Guide to Influence*, 2nd ed. (Cupertino, CA: Happy About, November 2012).

[5]"The Toolkit: Blame Frame vs. Aim Frame," Executive Advisory website, accessed May 6, 2017, http://www.theexecutiveadvisory.com/toolkit/blame_vs_aim.html.

[6]Zig Ziglar, *God's Way Is Still the Best Way* (Nashville: Thomas Nelson, 2007), 46.

[7]Malcolm Gladwell, *The Tipping Point: How Little Things Can Make a Big Difference* (New York: Little Brown, 2000), 12.

[8]Kirsten Helvey, "Don't Underestimate the Power of Lateral Career Moves for Professional Growth," *Harvard Business Review*, May 10, 2016, https://hbr.org/2016/05/dont-underestimate -the-power-of-lateral-career-moves-for-professional-growth.

Chapter 9

[1]Genie Z. Laborde, *Influencing with Integrity: Management Skills for Communication and Negotiation* (Palo Alto: Syntony, 1983).

Chapter 10

[1]Portions of the first half of this chapter are based on a white paper we wrote in 2014 and a *Harvard Business Review* article published that same year. Kathryn Heath, Jill Flynn, and Mary Davis Holt, *Why Meetings Matter Even More for Women* (Charlotte, NC: Flynn Heath Holt Leadership, 2014); Kathryn Heath, Jill Flynn, and Mary Davis Holt, "Women, Find Your Voice," *Harvard Business Review*, June 2014, https://hbr.org/2014/06/women-find-your-voice.

[2]Juliet Eilperin, "White House Women Want to Be in the Room Where It Happens," *Washington Post*, September 13, 2016, https://www.washingtonpost.com/news/powerpost/wp/2016/09/13 /white-house-women-are-now-in-the-room-where-it-happens/?utm_term=.0885ea9fda5d.

Acknowledgments

We are grateful to all the women—our mothers, sisters, daughters, friends, and colleagues—who have influenced us and inspired us. It is a long list of incredible people. We deeply appreciate the support you have given us as we have followed our dream of creating a firm, coaching women, writing articles and books, and, best of all, working for our vision of moving women leaders forward faster.

To the thousands of exceptional women our firm has coached and trained over the past sixteen years: You have trusted us and shared your stories and your lives with us, and we will never forget you. Our hopes and dreams for you are the reasons we wrote this book.

To our families—husbands, mothers, fathers, sisters, brothers, and grandchildren—but especially to our grown children, Angie, Kate, Taylor, Heath, David, Catie, and Mary Cameron: you inspire us to work hard for a better future.

To our incredible consultants, who facilitate our many leadership programs, workshops, and coaching: Thank you for your dedication and superb representation of Flynn Heath Holt in your far-flung travels to serve our clientele. Your experiences, wisdom, and coaching insights shared with us over the years have helped to supplement our own in this book. Plus, you are great fun to work with!

To the many business leaders who filled out our surveys or agreed to be interviewed: Thank you for the time you gave so generously to teach us so that we could in turn teach others. Your wisdom is evident in the pages of this book. We cannot name all of you, but you know who you are.

To the staff of Flynn Heath Holt: Thank you for your amazing teamwork and the long hours you have spent to grow our firm and make this book a reality.

Special kudos to Gary Applegate, Selene Butts, Kati Hollifield, Candy McCraven, Maggie Norris, Dahiana Pena, Wendy Pond, Tina Powell, Vicki Skipper, and Simone Williams. We couldn't have completed this book without the talent and efforts of each one of you. You are the best!

Special thanks go to Molly Beckert and Brian Collin for helping us to analyze our research data.

We also would like to thank all the people who have helped us day to day and made it possible for us to have the career and work we love.

To Anna Leinberger, our editor at Berrett-Koehler Publishers: thank you for helping us flesh out ideas and make *The Influence Effect* even more impactful.

Last but not least, we wish to express our heartfelt thanks to Jacque Murphy, our tireless collaborator and good friend, who has helped us with two books now: *Break Your Own Rules* and *The Influence Effect*. You served as our agent, connecting us with Berrett-Koehler Publishers. You helped us shape and hone our ideas and find our collective voice as authors, and you guided us through the entire writing process. We would not be in print without your great talent, extensive knowledge, and influence.

We extend gratitude to all of you.

Index

About the Authors

All four authors of *The Influence Effect: A New Path to Power for Women Leaders* are partners at Flynn Heath Holt Leadership (FHHL), a firm dedicated to moving women leaders forward faster. They are inspired by their Red Suit Vision, which calls for women to make up a minimum of 30 percent *of all top leadership positions in corporate America by the year 2025.*

Kathryn Heath is a founding partner at FHHL who develops leadership programs, coaches executives, and designs training. She specializes in identifying organizations' specific business targets through customized programs and working with executives and high-potential leaders at Fortune 500 companies. She coauthored *Break Your Own Rules: How to Change the Patterns of Thinking That Block Women's Paths to Power,* which landed on the best-seller lists of the *New York Times,* the *Wall Street Journal, USA Today,* and the *Washington Post.* Before she cofounded FHHL, Kathryn was senior vice president and director of First University at the nation's fourth-largest bank, First Union (now Wells Fargo), where her inventive and results-focused approach won her numerous awards in the field of learning and development.

Jill Flynn is a founding partner at FHHL and a coauthor of *Break Your Own Rules.* Her work with corporate clients results in higher retention and promotion rates of their women leaders. Jill is widely recognized for her coaching, training, speaking, and consulting expertise and has a roster of happy clients. She previously served as senior vice president at the nation's fourth-largest bank, First Union (now Wells Fargo), where she established their leadership development, diversity, organizational consulting, and employee satisfaction initiatives. As the corporation grew exponentially during her tenure, Jill and her team prepared a cadre of high-potential leaders to assume senior positions. Within a three-year timeframe, the number of women in these roles increased from 9 percent to 26 percent.

Mary Davis Holt, also a partner at FHHL and coauthor of *Break Your Own Rules*, is an in-demand speaker who shares her hard-won insights and promotes the firm's new rules for success to a wide range of audiences. Mary is also a sought-after facilitator and executive coach, and she works with companies to plan strategies that change the culture to support women leaders. Prior to joining FHHL, Mary held executive positions at Time Warner with oversight that ranged from finance to information technology, marketing, human resources, manufacturing, and distribution. She held a number of leadership roles in the publishing group, including senior executive vice president and chief operating officer of Time Life.

Diana Faison is a partner at FHHL, and she worked with the firm as a consultant for over ten years before her partnership. She began her career as a teacher of leadership development studies and a dean in student affairs at Queens University and the University of North Carolina–Charlotte. Over the span of her career, she has coached clients in a wide range of industries, including professional services, global real estate, financial services, software development, and health care. Diana is a sought-after keynote speaker on business leadership topics such as political savvy, brand, personal power, authentic leadership, and well-being.

For more information about the authors and Flynn Heath Holt Leadership, please visit www.FlynnHeath.com.

Berrett–Koehler
Publishers

Berrett-Koehler is an independent publisher dedicated to an ambitious mission: Connecting people and ideas to create a world that works for all.

We believe that the solutions to the world's problems will come from all of us, working at all levels: in our organizations, in our society, and in our own lives. Our BK Business books help people make their organizations more humane, democratic, diverse, and effective (we don't think there's any contradiction there). Our BK Currents books offer pathways to creating a more just, equitable, and sustainable society. Our BK Life books help people create positive change in their lives and align their personal practices with their aspirations for a better world.

All of our books are designed to bring people seeking positive change together around the ideas that empower them to see and shape the world in a new way.

And we strive to practice what we preach. At the core of our approach is Stewardship, a deep sense of responsibility to administer the company for the benefit of all of our stakeholder groups including authors, customers, employees, investors, service providers, and the communities and environment around us. Everything we do is built around this and our other key values of quality, partnership, inclusion, and sustainability.

This is why we are both a B-Corporation and a California Benefit Corporation—a certification and a for-profit legal status that require us to adhere to the highest standards for corporate, social, and environmental performance.

We are grateful to our readers, authors, and other friends of the company who consider themselves to be part of the BK Community. We hope that you, too, will join us in our mission.

A BK Business Book

We hope you enjoy this BK Business book. BK Business books pioneer new leadership and management practices and socially responsible approaches to business. They are designed to provide you with groundbreaking and practical tools to transform your work and organizations while upholding the triple bottom line of people, planet, and profits. High-five!

To find out more, visit **www.bkconnection.com.**

Berrett–Koehler
Publishers

Connecting people and ideas
to create a world that works for all

Dear Reader,

Thank you for picking up this book and joining our worldwide community of Berrett-Koehler readers. We share ideas that bring positive change into people's lives, organizations, and society.

To welcome you, we'd like to offer you a free e-book. You can pick from among twelve of our bestselling books by entering the promotional code **BKP92E** here: http://www.bkconnection.com/welcome.

When you claim your free e-book, we'll also send you a copy of our e-news-letter, the *BK Communiqué*. Although you're free to unsubscribe, there are many benefits to sticking around. In every issue of our newsletter you'll find

- A free e-book
- Tips from famous authors
- Discounts on spotlight titles
- Hilarious insider publishing news
- A chance to win a prize for answering a riddle

Best of all, our readers tell us, "Your newsletter is the only one I actually read." So claim your gift today, and please stay in touch!

Sincerely,

Charlotte Ashlock
Steward of the BK Website

Questions? Comments? Contact me at bkcommunity@bkpub.com.

MIX
Paper from
responsible sources
FSC® C002589

Certified

Corporation
bcorporation.net